MW01659866

Security Consultants
Complete Self-Assessment Guide

The guidance in this Self-Assessment is based on Security Consultants best practices and standards in business process architecture, design and quality management. The guidance is also based on the professional judgment of the individual collaborators listed in the Acknowledgments.

Notice of rights

You are licensed to use the Self-Assessment contents in your presentations and materials for internal use and customers without asking us - we are here to help.

All rights reserved for the book itself: this book may not be reproduced or transmitted in any form by any means, electronic, mechanical, photocopying, recording, or otherwise, without the prior written permission of the publisher.

The information in this book is distributed on an "As Is" basis without warranty. While every precaution has been taken in the preparation of he book, neither the author nor the publisher shall have any liability to any person or entity with respect to any loss or damage caused or alleged to be caused directly or indirectly by the instructions contained in this book or by the products described in it.

Trademarks

Many of the designations used by manufacturers and sellers to distinguish their products are claimed as trademarks. Where those designations appear in this book, and the publisher was aware of a trademark claim, the designations appear as requested by the owner of the trademark. All other product names and services identified throughout this book are used in editorial fashion only and for the benefit of such companies with no intention of infringement of the trademark. No such use, or the use of any trade name, is intended to convey endorsement or other affiliation with this book.

Copyright © by The Art of Service
http://theartofservice.com
service@theartofservice.com

Table of Contents

About The Art of Service

The Art of Service, Business Process Architects since 2000, is dedicated to helping stakeholders achieve excellence.

Defining, designing, creating, and implementing a process to solve a stakeholders challenge or meet an objective is the most valuable role... In EVERY group, company, organization and department.

Unless you're talking a one-time, single-use project, there should be a process. Whether that process is managed and implemented by humans, AI, or a combination of the two, it needs to be designed by someone with a complex enough perspective to ask the right questions.

Someone capable of asking the right questions and step back and say, 'What are we really trying to accomplish here? And is there a different way to look at it?'

With The Art of Service's Standard Requirements Self-Assessments, we empower people who can do just that — whether their title is marketer, entrepreneur, manager, salesperson, consultant, Business Process Manager, executive assistant, IT Manager, CIO etc... —they are the people who rule the future. They are people who watch the process as it happens, and ask the right questions to make the process work better.

Contact us when you need any support with this Self-Assessment and any help with templates, blue-prints and examples of standard documents you might need:

http://theartofservice.com
service@theartofservice.com

Acknowledgments

This checklist was developed under the auspices of The Art of Service, chaired by Gerardus Blokdyk.

Representatives from several client companies participated in the preparation of this Self-Assessment.

In addition, we are thankful for the design and printing services provided.

Included Resources - how to access

Included with your purchase of the book is the Security Consultants Self-Assessment Spreadsheet Dashboard which contains all questions and Self-Assessment areas and auto-generates insights, graphs, and project RACI planning - all with examples to get you started right away.

How? Simply send an email to
access@theartofservice.com
with this books' title in the subject to get the Security Consultants Self Assessment Tool right away.

You will receive the following contents with New and Updated specific criteria:

- The latest quick edition of the book in PDF
- The latest complete edition of the book in PDF, which criteria correspond to the criteria in...
- The Self-Assessment Excel Dashboard, and...
- Example pre-filled Self-Assessment Excel Dashboard to get familiar with results generation
- In-depth specific Checklists covering the topic
- Project management checklists and templates to assist with implementation

INCLUDES LIFETIME SELF ASSESSMENT UPDATES

Every self assessment comes with Lifetime Updates and Lifetime Free Updated Books. Lifetime Updates is an industry-first feature which allows you to receive verified self assessment updates, ensuring you always have the most accurate information at your fingertips.

Get it now- you will be glad you did - do it now, before you forget.

Send an email to **access@theartofservice.com** with this books' title in the subject to get the Security Consultants Self Assessment Tool right away.

Your feedback is invaluable to us

If you recently bought this book, we would love to hear from you! You can do this by writing a review on amazon (or the online store where you purchased this book) about your last purchase! As part of our continual service improvement process, we love to hear real client experiences and feedback.

How does it work?
To post a review on Amazon, just log in to your account and click on the Create Your Own Review button (under Customer Reviews) of the relevant product page. You can find examples of product reviews in Amazon. If you purchased from another online store, simply follow their procedures.

What happens when I submit my review?
Once you have submitted your review, send us an email at review@theartofservice.com with the link to your review so we can properly thank you for your feedback.

Purpose of this Self-Assessment

This Self-Assessment has been developed to improve understanding of the requirements and elements of Security Consultants, based on best practices and standards in business process architecture, design and quality management.

It is designed to allow for a rapid Self-Assessment to determine how closely existing management practices and procedures correspond to the elements of the Self-Assessment.

The criteria of requirements and elements of Security Consultants have been rephrased in the format of a Self-Assessment questionnaire, with a seven-criterion scoring system, as explained in this document.

In this format, even with limited background knowledge of

Security Consultants, a manager can quickly review existing operations to determine how they measure up to the standards. This in turn can serve as the starting point of a 'gap analysis' to identify management tools or system elements that might usefully be implemented in the organization to help improve overall performance.

How to use the Self-Assessment

On the following pages are a series of questions to identify to what extent your Security Consultants initiative is complete in comparison to the requirements set in standards.

To facilitate answering the questions, there is a space in front of each question to enter a score on a scale of '1' to '5'.

1 Strongly Disagree

2 Disagree

3 Neutral

4 Agree

5 Strongly Agree

Read the question and rate it with the following in front of mind:

**'In my belief,
the answer to this question is clearly defined'.**

There are two ways in which you can choose to interpret this statement;

1. how aware are you that the answer to the question is clearly defined
2. for more in-depth analysis you can choose to gather

evidence and confirm the answer to the question. This obviously will take more time, most Self-Assessment users opt for the first way to interpret the question and dig deeper later on based on the outcome of the overall Self-Assessment.

A score of '1' would mean that the answer is not clear at all, where a '5' would mean the answer is crystal clear and defined. Leave emtpy when the question is not applicable or you don't want to answer it, you can skip it without affecting your score. Write your score in the space provided.

After you have responded to all the appropriate statements in each section, compute your average score for that section, using the formula provided, and round to the nearest tenth. Then transfer to the corresponding spoke in the Security Consultants Scorecard on the second next page of the Self-Assessment.

Your completed Security Consultants Scorecard will give you a clear presentation of which Security Consultants areas need attention.

Security Consultants Scorecard Example

Example of how the finalized Scorecard can look like:

Security Consultants Scorecard

Your Scores:

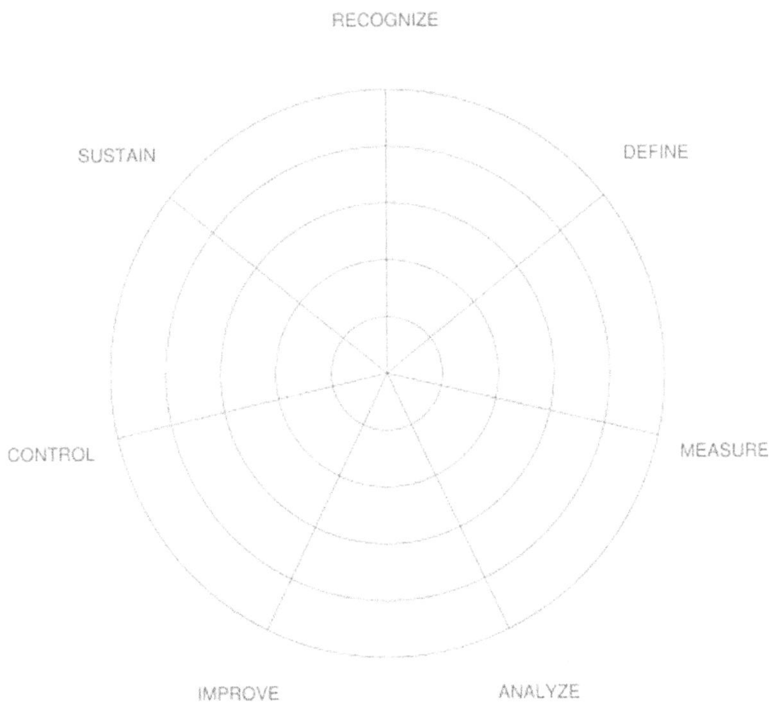

BEGINNING OF THE SELF-ASSESSMENT:

CRITERION #1: RECOGNIZE

INTENT: Be aware of the need for change. Recognize that there is an unfavorable variation, problem or symptom.

In my belief, the answer to this question is clearly defined:

5 Strongly Agree

4 Agree

3 Neutral

2 Disagree

1 Strongly Disagree

1. How are the security consultants's objectives aligned to the group's overall stakeholder strategy?
<--- Score

2. Looking at each person individually – does every one have the qualities which are needed to work in this group?
<--- Score

3. How do you identify the kinds of information that you will need?
<--- Score

4. What information do users need?
<--- Score

5. Which issues are too important to ignore?
<--- Score

6. What should be considered when identifying available resources, constraints, and deadlines?
<--- Score

7. What prevents you from making the changes you know will make you a more effective security consultants leader?
<--- Score

8. Do you recognize security consultants achievements?
<--- Score

9. How are you going to measure success?
<--- Score

10. Why the need?
<--- Score

11. What security consultants events should you attend?
<--- Score

12. Are there security consultants problems defined?
<--- Score

13. Are you dealing with any of the same issues today as yesterday? What can you do about this?
<--- Score

14. Who defines the rules in relation to any given issue?
<--- Score

15. What are your needs in relation to security consultants skills, labor, equipment, and markets?
<--- Score

16. Would you recognize a threat from the inside?
<--- Score

17. Will security consultants deliverables need to be tested and, if so, by whom?
<--- Score

18. Do you need different information or graphics?
<--- Score

19. Are your goals realistic? Do you need to redefine your problem? Perhaps the problem has changed or maybe you have reached your goal and need to set a new one?
<--- Score

20. What activities does the governance board need to consider?
<--- Score

21. What security consultants coordination do you need?
<--- Score

22. Does your organization need more security consultants education?
<--- Score

23. Can management personnel recognize the monetary benefit of security consultants?
<--- Score

24. What security consultants capabilities do you need?
<--- Score

25. What are the expected benefits of security consultants to the stakeholder?
<--- Score

26. Do you need to avoid or amend any security consultants activities?
<--- Score

27. As a sponsor, customer or management, how important is it to meet goals, objectives?
<--- Score

28. How do you assess your security consultants workforce capability and capacity needs, including skills, competencies, and staffing levels?
<--- Score

29. Does security consultants create potential expectations in other areas that need to be recognized and considered?
<--- Score

30. What needs to stay?

<--- Score

31. What do employees need in the short term?
<--- Score

32. What situation(s) led to this security consultants Self Assessment?
<--- Score

33. What tools and technologies are needed for a custom security consultants project?
<--- Score

34. What security consultants problem should be solved?
<--- Score

35. To what extent would your organization benefit from being recognized as a award recipient?
<--- Score

36. For your security consultants project, identify and describe the business environment, is there more than one layer to the business environment?
<--- Score

37. Will it solve real problems?
<--- Score

38. Does the problem have ethical dimensions?
<--- Score

39. What is the extent or complexity of the security consultants problem?
<--- Score

40. How do you take a forward-looking perspective in identifying security consultants research related to market response and models?
<--- Score

41. How are training requirements identified?
<--- Score

42. What creative shifts do you need to take?
<--- Score

43. Who are your key stakeholders who need to sign off?
<--- Score

44. What problems are you facing and how do you consider security consultants will circumvent those obstacles?
<--- Score

45. When a security consultants manager recognizes a problem, what options are available?
<--- Score

46. Are employees recognized or rewarded for performance that demonstrates the highest levels of integrity?
<--- Score

47. Did you miss any major security consultants issues?
<--- Score

48. Who else hopes to benefit from it?
<--- Score

49. Who needs to know about security consultants?
<--- Score

50. What is the problem and/or vulnerability?
<--- Score

51. Which information does the security consultants business case need to include?
<--- Score

52. Consider your own security consultants project, what types of organizational problems do you think might be causing or affecting your problem, based on the work done so far?
<--- Score

53. Are losses recognized in a timely manner?
<--- Score

54. What else needs to be measured?
<--- Score

55. What are the clients issues and concerns?
<--- Score

56. What is the recognized need?
<--- Score

57. Are there any revenue recognition issues?
<--- Score

58. What does security consultants success mean to the stakeholders?
<--- Score

59. What do you need to start doing?

<--- Score

60. To what extent does each concerned units management team recognize security consultants as an effective investment?
<--- Score

61. What needs to be done?
<--- Score

62. How does it fit into your organizational needs and tasks?
<--- Score

63. How do you recognize an objection?
<--- Score

64. What would happen if security consultants weren't done?
<--- Score

65. Whom do you really need or want to serve?
<--- Score

66. What is the problem or issue?
<--- Score

67. Is the need for organizational change recognized?
<--- Score

68. How do you identify subcontractor relationships?
<--- Score

69. What are the stakeholder objectives to be achieved with security consultants?
<--- Score

70. Who should resolve the security consultants issues?
<--- Score

71. How can auditing be a preventative security measure?
<--- Score

72. Do you have/need 24-hour access to key personnel?
<--- Score

73. What training and capacity building actions are needed to implement proposed reforms?
<--- Score

74. Think about the people you identified for your security consultants project and the project responsibilities you would assign to them, what kind of training do you think they would need to perform these responsibilities effectively?
<--- Score

75. What are the security consultants resources needed?
<--- Score

76. How much are sponsors, customers, partners, stakeholders involved in security consultants? In other words, what are the risks, if security consultants does not deliver successfully?
<--- Score

77. Where do you need to exercise leadership?
<--- Score

78. Is it clear when you think of the day ahead of you what activities and tasks you need to complete?
<--- Score

79. Where is training needed?
<--- Score

80. Are there recognized security consultants problems?
<--- Score

81. How many trainings, in total, are needed?
<--- Score

82. What is the smallest subset of the problem you can usefully solve?
<--- Score

83. Who needs to know?
<--- Score

84. Is it needed?
<--- Score

85. What is the security consultants problem definition? What do you need to resolve?
<--- Score

86. Are employees recognized for desired behaviors?
<--- Score

87. What extra resources will you need?
<--- Score

88. What are the timeframes required to resolve each of the issues/problems?
<--- Score

89. Is the quality assurance team identified?
<--- Score

90. Are controls defined to recognize and contain problems?
<--- Score

91. Do you know what you need to know about security consultants?
<--- Score

92. Why is this needed?
<--- Score

93. Who needs budgets?
<--- Score

94. Are there regulatory / compliance issues?
<--- Score

95. How do you recognize an security consultants objection?
<--- Score

96. Are there any specific expectations or concerns about the security consultants team, security consultants itself?
<--- Score

97. Have you identified your security consultants key performance indicators?
<--- Score

98. Are problem definition and motivation clearly presented?
<--- Score

99. What are the minority interests and what amount of minority interests can be recognized?
<--- Score

100. Will a response program recognize when a crisis occurs and provide some level of response?
<--- Score

Add up total points for this section:
_____ = Total points for this section

Divided by: ______ (number of statements answered) = ______ Average score for this section

Transfer your score to the security consultants Index at the beginning of the Self-Assessment.

CRITERION #2: DEFINE:

INTENT: Formulate the stakeholder problem. Define the problem, needs and objectives.

In my belief, the answer to this question is clearly defined:

5 Strongly Agree

4 Agree

3 Neutral

2 Disagree

1 Strongly Disagree

1. What sort of initial information to gather?
<--- Score

2. Are required metrics defined, what are they?
<--- Score

3. How have you defined all security consultants requirements first?
<--- Score

4. Is security consultants linked to key stakeholder goals and objectives?
<--- Score

5. What are the Roles and Responsibilities for each team member and its leadership? Where is this documented?
<--- Score

6. Are customer(s) identified and segmented according to their different needs and requirements?
<--- Score

7. Are different versions of process maps needed to account for the different types of inputs?
<--- Score

8. What customer feedback methods were used to solicit their input?
<--- Score

9. Has a project plan, Gantt chart, or similar been developed/completed?
<--- Score

10. Are there different segments of customers?
<--- Score

11. What is the context?
<--- Score

12. Do the problem and goal statements meet the SMART criteria (specific, measurable, attainable, relevant, and time-bound)?
<--- Score

13. What defines best in class?
<--- Score

14. Is the team equipped with available and reliable resources?
<--- Score

15. What scope to assess?
<--- Score

16. What happens if security consultants's scope changes?
<--- Score

17. How are consistent security consultants definitions important?
<--- Score

18. Do you all define security consultants in the same way?
<--- Score

19. Are audit criteria, scope, frequency and methods defined?
<--- Score

20. Are approval levels defined for contracts and supplements to contracts?
<--- Score

21. Are the security consultants requirements complete?
<--- Score

22. What are the record-keeping requirements of

security consultants activities?
<--- Score

23. What are the dynamics of the communication plan?
<--- Score

24. What system do you use for gathering security consultants information?
<--- Score

25. What is out of scope?
<--- Score

26. Has a team charter been developed and communicated?
<--- Score

27. What baselines are required to be defined and managed?
<--- Score

28. What is the scope of the security consultants effort?
<--- Score

29. Is the improvement team aware of the different versions of a process: what they think it is vs. what it actually is vs. what it should be vs. what it could be?
<--- Score

30. Are there any constraints known that bear on the ability to perform security consultants work? How is the team addressing them?
<--- Score

31. Has a high-level 'as is' process map been completed, verified and validated?
<--- Score

32. Has a security consultants requirement not been met?
<--- Score

33. What sources do you use to gather information for a security consultants study?
<--- Score

34. Are resources adequate for the scope?
<--- Score

35. What is in the scope and what is not in scope?
<--- Score

36. What is the scope of the security consultants work?
<--- Score

37. What are (control) requirements for security consultants Information?
<--- Score

38. The political context: who holds power?
<--- Score

39. Has/have the customer(s) been identified?
<--- Score

40. Is the team formed and are team leaders (Coaches and Management Leads) assigned?
<--- Score

41. Is the team sponsored by a champion or stakeholder leader?
<--- Score

42. Are accountability and ownership for security consultants clearly defined?
<--- Score

43. Is there a clear security consultants case definition?
<--- Score

44. What is the definition of success?
<--- Score

45. Is there regularly 100% attendance at the team meetings? If not, have appointed substitutes attended to preserve cross-functionality and full representation?
<--- Score

46. What are the security consultants use cases?
<--- Score

47. How do you build the right business case?
<--- Score

48. Does the scope remain the same?
<--- Score

49. What is the scope?
<--- Score

50. What is the worst case scenario?
<--- Score

51. Is there a completed, verified, and validated high-level 'as is' (not 'should be' or 'could be') stakeholder process map?
<--- Score

52. Who approved the security consultants scope?
<--- Score

53. How is the team tracking and documenting its work?
<--- Score

54. Is there any additional security consultants definition of success?
<--- Score

55. Is special security consultants user knowledge required?
<--- Score

56. When is/was the security consultants start date?
<--- Score

57. Is it clearly defined in and to your organization what you do?
<--- Score

58. Who are the security consultants improvement team members, including Management Leads and Coaches?
<--- Score

59. What security consultants requirements should be gathered?
<--- Score

60. How and when will the baselines be defined?
<--- Score

61. Has everyone on the team, including the team leaders, been properly trained?
<--- Score

62. Is there a completed SIPOC representation, describing the Suppliers, Inputs, Process, Outputs, and Customers?
<--- Score

63. How do you keep key subject matter experts in the loop?
<--- Score

64. How do you gather requirements?
<--- Score

65. How do you manage scope?
<--- Score

66. Is security consultants currently on schedule according to the plan?
<--- Score

67. Why are you doing security consultants and what is the scope?
<--- Score

68. Is full participation by members in regularly held team meetings guaranteed?
<--- Score

69. What is the scope of security consultants?
<--- Score

70. Is the security consultants scope complete and appropriately sized?
<--- Score

71. What are the security consultants tasks and definitions?
<--- Score

72. When is the estimated completion date?
<--- Score

73. How would you define security consultants leadership?
<--- Score

74. Have all basic functions of security consultants been defined?
<--- Score

75. What information do you gather?
<--- Score

76. Is the security consultants scope manageable?
<--- Score

77. Are task requirements clearly defined?
<--- Score

78. What critical content must be communicated – who, what, when, where, and how?
<--- Score

79. Where can you gather more information?
<--- Score

80. Has the direction changed at all during the course of security consultants? If so, when did it change and why?
<--- Score

81. What are the boundaries of the scope? What is in bounds and what is not? What is the start point? What is the stop point?
<--- Score

82. How do you manage unclear security consultants requirements?
<--- Score

83. How do you manage changes in security consultants requirements?
<--- Score

84. What information should you gather?
<--- Score

85. Will team members perform security consultants work when assigned and in a timely fashion?
<--- Score

86. How can the value of security consultants be defined?
<--- Score

87. Have the customer needs been translated into specific, measurable requirements? How?
<--- Score

88. Who is gathering security consultants information?
<--- Score

89. What constraints exist that might impact the team?
<--- Score

90. In what way can you redefine the criteria of choice clients have in your category in your favor?
<--- Score

91. How do you gather the stories?
<--- Score

92. Is scope creep really all bad news?
<--- Score

93. Are improvement team members fully trained on security consultants?
<--- Score

94. How did the security consultants manager receive input to the development of a security consultants improvement plan and the estimated completion dates/times of each activity?
<--- Score

95. What is in scope?
<--- Score

96. Is there a security consultants management charter, including stakeholder case, problem and goal statements, scope, milestones, roles and responsibilities, communication plan?
<--- Score

97. Are roles and responsibilities formally defined?
<--- Score

98. Is data collected and displayed to better understand customer(s) critical needs and requirements.
<--- Score

99. Scope of sensitive information?
<--- Score

100. Has the security consultants work been fairly and/or equitably divided and delegated among team members who are qualified and capable to perform the work? Has everyone contributed?
<--- Score

101. Who is gathering information?
<--- Score

102. Has your scope been defined?
<--- Score

103. What key stakeholder process output measure(s) does security consultants leverage and how?
<--- Score

104. How do you hand over security consultants context?
<--- Score

105. Have specific policy objectives been defined?
<--- Score

106. Do you have organizational privacy requirements?
<--- Score

107. What are the tasks and definitions?
<--- Score

108. Is the scope of security consultants defined?
<--- Score

109. Do you have a security consultants success story or case study ready to tell and share?
<--- Score

110. How will the security consultants team and the group measure complete success of security consultants?
<--- Score

111. What are the compelling stakeholder reasons for embarking on security consultants?
<--- Score

112. Is there a critical path to deliver security consultants results?
<--- Score

113. How do you gather security consultants requirements?
<--- Score

114. What gets examined?
<--- Score

115. Have all of the relationships been defined properly?
<--- Score

116. Is the team adequately staffed with the desired cross-functionality? If not, what additional resources

are available to the team?
<--- Score

117. What scope do you want your strategy to cover?
<--- Score

118. What was the context?
<--- Score

119. How do you think the partners involved in security consultants would have defined success?
<--- Score

120. What are the requirements for audit information?
<--- Score

121. How often are the team meetings?
<--- Score

122. What security consultants services do you require?
<--- Score

123. Are the security consultants requirements testable?
<--- Score

124. When are meeting minutes sent out? Who is on the distribution list?
<--- Score

125. What are the rough order estimates on cost savings/opportunities that security consultants brings?
<--- Score

126. What would be the goal or target for a security consultants's improvement team?
<--- Score

127. What is the definition of security consultants excellence?
<--- Score

128. Has anyone else (internal or external to the group) attempted to solve this problem or a similar one before? If so, what knowledge can be leveraged from these previous efforts?
<--- Score

129. Will team members regularly document their security consultants work?
<--- Score

130. How was the 'as is' process map developed, reviewed, verified and validated?
<--- Score

131. Will a security consultants production readiness review be required?
<--- Score

132. Does the team have regular meetings?
<--- Score

133. Is security consultants required?
<--- Score

134. How do you catch security consultants definition inconsistencies?
<--- Score

135. Is the current 'as is' process being followed? If not, what are the discrepancies?
<--- Score

136. How does the security consultants manager ensure against scope creep?
<--- Score

137. How will variation in the actual durations of each activity be dealt with to ensure that the expected security consultants results are met?
<--- Score

138. What is a worst-case scenario for losses?
<--- Score

139. What specifically is the problem? Where does it occur? When does it occur? What is its extent?
<--- Score

140. Has the improvement team collected the 'voice of the customer' (obtained feedback – qualitative and quantitative)?
<--- Score

141. If substitutes have been appointed, have they been briefed on the security consultants goals and received regular communications as to the progress to date?
<--- Score

Add up total points for this section:
_____ = Total points for this section

Divided by: ______ (number of

statements answered) = ______
Average score for this section

Transfer your score to the security consultants Index at the beginning of the Self-Assessment.

CRITERION #3: MEASURE:

INTENT: Gather the correct data. Measure the current performance and evolution of the situation.

In my belief, the answer to this question is clearly defined:

5 Strongly Agree

4 Agree

3 Neutral

2 Disagree

1 Strongly Disagree

1. What are the strategic priorities for this year?
<--- Score

2. What disadvantage does this cause for the user?
<--- Score

3. What are your customers expectations and measures?
<--- Score

4. Are actual costs in line with budgeted costs?
<--- Score

5. What is an unallowable cost?
<--- Score

6. Is there an opportunity to verify requirements?
<--- Score

7. What causes innovation to fail or succeed in your organization?
<--- Score

8. Are there measurements based on task performance?
<--- Score

9. What are the uncertainties surrounding estimates of impact?
<--- Score

10. What is your security consultants quality cost segregation study?
<--- Score

11. How do you quantify and qualify impacts?
<--- Score

12. How much does it cost?
<--- Score

13. How is progress measured?
<--- Score

14. What do you measure and why?

<--- Score

15. What drives O&M cost?
<--- Score

16. What methods are feasible and acceptable to estimate the impact of reforms?
<--- Score

17. What does a Test Case verify?
<--- Score

18. Have you included everything in your security consultants cost models?
<--- Score

19. What happens if cost savings do not materialize?
<--- Score

20. Are missed security consultants opportunities costing your organization money?
<--- Score

21. How frequently do you verify your security consultants strategy?
<--- Score

22. Does a security consultants quantification method exist?
<--- Score

23. Where is the cost?
<--- Score

24. What is the cost of rework?
<--- Score

25. How do you prevent mis-estimating cost?
<--- Score

26. Do you have an issue in getting priority?
<--- Score

27. Which security consultants impacts are significant?
<--- Score

28. How are measurements made?
<--- Score

29. How will the security consultants data be analyzed?
<--- Score

30. Which costs should be taken into account?
<--- Score

31. What are the costs?
<--- Score

32. What potential environmental factors impact the security consultants effort?
<--- Score

33. The approach of traditional security consultants works for detail complexity but is focused on a systematic approach rather than an understanding of the nature of systems themselves, what approach will permit your organization to deal with the kind of unpredictable emergent behaviors that dynamic complexity can introduce?
<--- Score

34. Are supply costs steady or fluctuating?
<--- Score

35. What are your primary costs, revenues, assets?
<--- Score

36. What is the cause of any security consultants gaps?
<--- Score

37. What could cause delays in the schedule?
<--- Score

38. Will security consultants have an impact on current business continuity, disaster recovery processes and/or infrastructure?
<--- Score

39. Are the security consultants benefits worth its costs?
<--- Score

40. How will measures be used to manage and adapt?
<--- Score

41. Where is it measured?
<--- Score

42. Did you tackle the cause or the symptom?
<--- Score

43. How do you measure efficient delivery of security consultants services?
<--- Score

44. How do you focus on what is right -not who is right?
<--- Score

45. How will you measure success?
<--- Score

46. Are there competing security consultants priorities?
<--- Score

47. Does the security consultants task fit the client's priorities?
<--- Score

48. Do you have any cost security consultants limitation requirements?
<--- Score

49. Who is involved in verifying compliance?
<--- Score

50. How do you stay flexible and focused to recognize larger security consultants results?
<--- Score

51. What do people want to verify?
<--- Score

52. Are security consultants vulnerabilities categorized and prioritized?
<--- Score

53. Where can you go to verify the info?
<--- Score

54. How is performance measured?
<--- Score

55. What does losing customers cost your organization?
<--- Score

56. Is the solution cost-effective?
<--- Score

57. How do you measure success?
<--- Score

58. What can be used to verify compliance?
<--- Score

59. What are the costs of reform?
<--- Score

60. Are indirect costs charged to the security consultants program?
<--- Score

61. Do you verify that corrective actions were taken?
<--- Score

62. What are the operational costs after security consultants deployment?
<--- Score

63. What are you verifying?
<--- Score

64. What is the total cost related to deploying security consultants, including any consulting or professional

services?
<--- Score

65. What tests verify requirements?
<--- Score

66. How do you verify performance?
<--- Score

67. How can you measure the performance?
<--- Score

68. Is the cost worth the security consultants effort ?
<--- Score

69. What does your operating model cost?
<--- Score

70. Has a cost center been established?
<--- Score

71. When are costs are incurred?
<--- Score

72. How do you aggregate measures across priorities?
<--- Score

73. How sensitive must the security consultants strategy be to cost?
<--- Score

74. Are you able to realize any cost savings?
<--- Score

75. How do you verify security consultants

completeness and accuracy?
<--- Score

76. Who should receive measurement reports?
<--- Score

77. Are you taking your company in the direction of better and revenue or cheaper and cost?
<--- Score

78. Have you made assumptions about the shape of the future, particularly its impact on your customers and competitors?
<--- Score

79. What measurements are being captured?
<--- Score

80. How do you verify your resources?
<--- Score

81. How do you measure variability?
<--- Score

82. How do you verify and develop ideas and innovations?
<--- Score

83. Is it possible to estimate the impact of unanticipated complexity such as wrong or failed assumptions, feedback, etcetera on proposed reforms?
<--- Score

84. What evidence is there and what is measured?
<--- Score

85. What are the security consultants key cost drivers?
<--- Score

86. Are there any easy-to-implement alternatives to security consultants? Sometimes other solutions are available that do not require the cost implications of a full-blown project?
<--- Score

87. What is measured? Why?
<--- Score

88. Do the benefits outweigh the costs?
<--- Score

89. How are costs allocated?
<--- Score

90. Is a follow-up focused external security consultants review required?
<--- Score

91. What are your key security consultants organizational performance measures, including key short and longer-term financial measures?
<--- Score

92. How can you reduce costs?
<--- Score

93. What are the types and number of measures to use?
<--- Score

94. What would it cost to replace your technology?

<--- Score

95. What is your decision requirements diagram?
<--- Score

96. What are hidden security consultants quality costs?
<--- Score

97. What are allowable costs?
<--- Score

98. Do you aggressively reward and promote the people who have the biggest impact on creating excellent security consultants services/products?
<--- Score

99. What details are required of the security consultants cost structure?
<--- Score

100. What are your operating costs?
<--- Score

101. Do you effectively measure and reward individual and team performance?
<--- Score

102. Have design-to-cost goals been established?
<--- Score

103. How do you verify the authenticity of the data and information used?
<--- Score

104. Why a security consultants focus?

<--- Score

105. What are the costs and benefits?
<--- Score

106. How can you measure security consultants in a systematic way?
<--- Score

107. How do your measurements capture actionable security consultants information for use in exceeding your customers expectations and securing your customers engagement?
<--- Score

108. How can you reduce the costs of obtaining inputs?
<--- Score

109. Are the measurements objective?
<--- Score

110. What relevant entities could be measured?
<--- Score

111. How to cause the change?
<--- Score

112. What is the root cause(s) of the problem?
<--- Score

113. What does verifying compliance entail?
<--- Score

114. What are the costs of delaying security consultants action?

<--- Score

115. What causes extra work or rework?
<--- Score

116. When a disaster occurs, who gets priority?
<--- Score

117. When should you bother with diagrams?
<--- Score

118. How will success or failure be measured?
<--- Score

119. Do you have a flow diagram of what happens?
<--- Score

120. How will costs be allocated?
<--- Score

121. How will you measure your security consultants effectiveness?
<--- Score

122. Why do the measurements/indicators matter?
<--- Score

123. How do you verify and validate the security consultants data?
<--- Score

124. Was a business case (cost/benefit) developed?
<--- Score

125. How do you verify if security consultants is built right?

<--- Score

126. How do you measure lifecycle phases?
<--- Score

127. How will effects be measured?
<--- Score

128. Who pays the cost?
<--- Score

129. What is the total fixed cost?
<--- Score

130. Why do you expend time and effort to implement measurement, for whom?
<--- Score

131. What measurements are possible, practicable and meaningful?
<--- Score

132. Are the units of measure consistent?
<--- Score

133. How are you verifying it?
<--- Score

134. How do you verify the security consultants requirements quality?
<--- Score

135. How do you control the overall costs of your work processes?
<--- Score

Add up total points for this section:
_____ = Total points for this section

Divided by: ______ (number of statements answered) = ______
Average score for this section

Transfer your score to the security consultants Index at the beginning of the Self-Assessment.

CRITERION #4: ANALYZE:

INTENT: Analyze causes, assumptions and hypotheses.

In my belief, the answer to this question is clearly defined:

5 Strongly Agree

4 Agree

3 Neutral

2 Disagree

1 Strongly Disagree

1. What training and qualifications will you need?
<--- Score

2. Have the problem and goal statements been updated to reflect the additional knowledge gained from the analyze phase?
<--- Score

3. What quality tools were used to get through the analyze phase?

<--- Score

4. What internal processes need improvement?
<--- Score

5. How is security consultants data gathered?
<--- Score

6. What are the revised rough estimates of the financial savings/opportunity for security consultants improvements?
<--- Score

7. Were there any improvement opportunities identified from the process analysis?
<--- Score

8. Is the final output clearly identified?
<--- Score

9. What data do you need to collect?
<--- Score

10. What are the best opportunities for value improvement?
<--- Score

11. What were the crucial 'moments of truth' on the process map?
<--- Score

12. Is pre-qualification of suppliers carried out?
<--- Score

13. What are the necessary qualifications?
<--- Score

14. What are your current levels and trends in key security consultants measures or indicators of product and process performance that are important to and directly serve your customers?
<--- Score

15. How does the organization define, manage, and improve its security consultants processes?
<--- Score

16. What other organizational variables, such as reward systems or communication systems, affect the performance of this security consultants process?
<--- Score

17. What are the personnel training and qualifications required?
<--- Score

18. What process improvements will be needed?
<--- Score

19. Was a detailed process map created to amplify critical steps of the 'as is' stakeholder process?
<--- Score

20. Think about the functions involved in your security consultants project, what processes flow from these functions?
<--- Score

21. Do quality systems drive continuous improvement?
<--- Score

22. Do staff qualifications match your project?
<--- Score

23. How do you ensure that the security consultants opportunity is realistic?
<--- Score

24. How will the security consultants data be captured?
<--- Score

25. Who qualifies to gain access to data?
<--- Score

26. What tools were used to generate the list of possible causes?
<--- Score

27. How do you identify specific security consultants investment opportunities and emerging trends?
<--- Score

28. What output to create?
<--- Score

29. Is data and process analysis, root cause analysis and quantifying the gap/opportunity in place?
<--- Score

30. An organizationally feasible system request is one that considers the mission, goals and objectives of the organization, key questions are: is the security consultants solution request practical and will it solve a problem or take

advantage of an opportunity to achieve company goals?
<--- Score

31. How do you define collaboration and team output?
<--- Score

32. Is there an established change management process?
<--- Score

33. What qualifications are needed?
<--- Score

34. Do you have the authority to produce the output?
<--- Score

35. Has an output goal been set?
<--- Score

36. What are your security consultants processes?
<--- Score

37. What is the oversight process?
<--- Score

38. Has data output been validated?
<--- Score

39. Have any additional benefits been identified that will result from closing all or most of the gaps?
<--- Score

40. Do your contracts/agreements contain data security obligations?

<--- Score

41. What are your best practices for minimizing security consultants project risk, while demonstrating incremental value and quick wins throughout the security consultants project lifecycle?
<--- Score

42. Who owns what data?
<--- Score

43. What is the Value Stream Mapping?
<--- Score

44. What security consultants metrics are outputs of the process?
<--- Score

45. Are you missing security consultants opportunities?
<--- Score

46. Are all staff in core security consultants subjects Highly Qualified?
<--- Score

47. Are security consultants changes recognized early enough to be approved through the regular process?
<--- Score

48. What conclusions were drawn from the team's data collection and analysis? How did the team reach these conclusions?
<--- Score

49. What, related to, security consultants processes

does your organization outsource?
<--- Score

50. Do several people in different organizational units assist with the security consultants process?
<--- Score

51. What did the team gain from developing a sub-process map?
<--- Score

52. Are gaps between current performance and the goal performance identified?
<--- Score

53. What methods do you use to gather security consultants data?
<--- Score

54. What are your current levels and trends in key measures or indicators of security consultants product and process performance that are important to and directly serve your customers? How do these results compare with the performance of your competitors and other organizations with similar offerings?
<--- Score

55. Identify an operational issue in your organization, for example, could a particular task be done more quickly or more efficiently by security consultants?
<--- Score

56. What are evaluation criteria for the output?
<--- Score

57. What is the complexity of the output produced?
<--- Score

58. How do you implement and manage your work processes to ensure that they meet design requirements?
<--- Score

59. Are all team members qualified for all tasks?
<--- Score

60. Which security consultants data should be retained?
<--- Score

61. What are the security consultants business drivers?
<--- Score

62. Who is involved with workflow mapping?
<--- Score

63. How has the security consultants data been gathered?
<--- Score

64. What does the data say about the performance of the stakeholder process?
<--- Score

65. Where can you get qualified talent today?
<--- Score

66. What successful thing are you doing today that may be blinding you to new growth opportunities?
<--- Score

67. Were Pareto charts (or similar) used to portray the 'heavy hitters' (or key sources of variation)?
<--- Score

68. What resources go in to get the desired output?
<--- Score

69. How is the security consultants Value Stream Mapping managed?
<--- Score

70. How do you promote understanding that opportunity for improvement is not criticism of the status quo, or the people who created the status quo?
<--- Score

71. How often will data be collected for measures?
<--- Score

72. Is the performance gap determined?
<--- Score

73. Is there a strict change management process?
<--- Score

74. Should you invest in industry-recognized qualifications?
<--- Score

75. What other jobs or tasks affect the performance of the steps in the security consultants process?
<--- Score

76. Was a cause-and-effect diagram used to explore

the different types of causes (or sources of variation)?
<--- Score

77. Who is involved in the management review process?
<--- Score

78. How is the data gathered?
<--- Score

79. Did any additional data need to be collected?
<--- Score

80. What is the output?
<--- Score

81. How are outputs preserved and protected?
<--- Score

82. Is the security consultants process severely broken such that a re-design is necessary?
<--- Score

83. Where is the data coming from to measure compliance?
<--- Score

84. What qualifications are necessary?
<--- Score

85. How many input/output points does it require?
<--- Score

86. Who gets your output?
<--- Score

87. What were the financial benefits resulting from any 'ground fruit or low-hanging fruit' (quick fixes)?
<--- Score

88. What tools were used to narrow the list of possible causes?
<--- Score

89. Do your leaders quickly bounce back from setbacks?
<--- Score

90. How can risk management be tied procedurally to process elements?
<--- Score

91. What are your outputs?
<--- Score

92. How much data can be collected in the given timeframe?
<--- Score

93. Is the suppliers process defined and controlled?
<--- Score

94. What qualifications do security consultants leaders need?
<--- Score

95. Record-keeping requirements flow from the records needed as inputs, outputs, controls and for transformation of a security consultants process, are the records needed as inputs to the security consultants process available?
<--- Score

96. How do you use security consultants data and information to support organizational decision making and innovation?
<--- Score

97. What kind of crime could a potential new hire have committed that would not only not disqualify him/her from being hired by your organization, but would actually indicate that he/she might be a particularly good fit?
<--- Score

98. Do you understand your management processes today?
<--- Score

99. How was the detailed process map generated, verified, and validated?
<--- Score

100. How is the way you as the leader think and process information affecting your organizational culture?
<--- Score

101. What is your organizations system for selecting qualified vendors?
<--- Score

102. What controls do you have in place to protect data?
<--- Score

103. What types of data do your security consultants indicators require?

<--- Score

104. Who will gather what data?
<--- Score

105. Is the gap/opportunity displayed and communicated in financial terms?
<--- Score

106. What qualifies as competition?
<--- Score

107. How difficult is it to qualify what security consultants ROI is?
<--- Score

108. What do you need to qualify?
<--- Score

109. How do your work systems and key work processes relate to and capitalize on your core competencies?
<--- Score

110. How do you measure the operational performance of your key work systems and processes, including productivity, cycle time, and other appropriate measures of process effectiveness, efficiency, and innovation?
<--- Score

111. Were any designed experiments used to generate additional insight into the data analysis?
<--- Score

112. How will the change process be managed?

<--- Score

113. Think about some of the processes you undertake within your organization, which do you own?
<--- Score

114. What is the security consultants Driver?
<--- Score

115. Are your outputs consistent?
<--- Score

116. Is the required security consultants data gathered?
<--- Score

117. What are your key performance measures or indicators and in-process measures for the control and improvement of your security consultants processes?
<--- Score

118. What process should you select for improvement?
<--- Score

119. What information qualified as important?
<--- Score

120. A compounding model resolution with available relevant data can often provide insight towards a solution methodology; which security consultants models, tools and techniques are necessary?
<--- Score

121. Have you defined which data is gathered how?
<--- Score

122. What is your organizations process which leads to recognition of value generation?
<--- Score

123. Do your employees have the opportunity to do what they do best everyday?
<--- Score

124. Did any value-added analysis or 'lean thinking' take place to identify some of the gaps shown on the 'as is' process map?
<--- Score

125. Do you, as a leader, bounce back quickly from setbacks?
<--- Score

126. How do mission and objectives affect the security consultants processes of your organization?
<--- Score

127. What is the cost of poor quality as supported by the team's analysis?
<--- Score

128. What qualifications and skills do you need?
<--- Score

Add up total points for this section:
_____ = Total points for this section

Divided by: ______ (number of

statements answered) = ______
Average score for this section

Transfer your score to the security consultants Index at the beginning of the Self-Assessment.

CRITERION #5: IMPROVE:

INTENT: Develop a practical solution. Innovate, establish and test the solution and to measure the results.

In my belief, the answer to this question is clearly defined:

5 Strongly Agree

4 Agree

3 Neutral

2 Disagree

1 Strongly Disagree

1. Who controls the risk?
<--- Score

2. Was a security consultants charter developed?
<--- Score

3. What needs improvement? Why?
<--- Score

4. Where do you need security consultants improvement?
<--- Score

5. What is security consultants's impact on utilizing the best solution(s)?
<--- Score

6. Can you identify any significant risks or exposures to security consultants third- parties (vendors, service providers, alliance partners etc) that concern you?
<--- Score

7. Where do the security consultants decisions reside?
<--- Score

8. To what extent does management recognize security consultants as a tool to increase the results?
<--- Score

9. Are the best solutions selected?
<--- Score

10. Who are the people involved in developing and implementing security consultants?
<--- Score

11. What criteria will you use to assess your security consultants risks?
<--- Score

12. What is the security consultants's sustainability risk?
<--- Score

13. Are improved process ('should be') maps modified based on pilot data and analysis?
<--- Score

14. What lessons, if any, from a pilot were incorporated into the design of the full-scale solution?
<--- Score

15. Do you need to do a usability evaluation?
<--- Score

16. What went well, what should change, what can improve?
<--- Score

17. Does a good decision guarantee a good outcome?
<--- Score

18. What are the affordable security consultants risks?
<--- Score

19. Have you identified breakpoints and/or risk tolerances that will trigger broad consideration of a potential need for intervention or modification of strategy?
<--- Score

20. How does the solution remove the key sources of issues discovered in the analyze phase?
<--- Score

21. Is a contingency plan established?
<--- Score

22. Is there a cost/benefit analysis of optimal solution(s)?

<--- Score

23. Do you combine technical expertise with business knowledge and security consultants Key topics include lifecycles, development approaches, requirements and how to make a business case?
<--- Score

24. Have you achieved security consultants improvements?
<--- Score

25. What attendant changes will need to be made to ensure that the solution is successful?
<--- Score

26. How can skill-level changes improve security consultants?
<--- Score

27. security consultants risk decisions: whose call Is It?
<--- Score

28. What is the team's contingency plan for potential problems occurring in implementation?
<--- Score

29. Risk events: what are the things that could go wrong?
<--- Score

30. How did the team generate the list of possible solutions?
<--- Score

31. Which of the recognised risks out of all risks can be

most likely transferred?
<--- Score

32. Who will be using the results of the measurement activities?
<--- Score

33. How do you deal with security consultants risk?
<--- Score

34. How will the team or the process owner(s) monitor the implementation plan to see that it is working as intended?
<--- Score

35. What security consultants improvements can be made?
<--- Score

36. At what point will vulnerability assessments be performed once security consultants is put into production (e.g., ongoing Risk Management after implementation)?
<--- Score

37. Was a pilot designed for the proposed solution(s)?
<--- Score

38. How significant is the improvement in the eyes of the end user?
<--- Score

39. What to do with the results or outcomes of measurements?
<--- Score

40. How do you manage security consultants risk?
<--- Score

41. Is the security consultants risk managed?
<--- Score

42. Who are the key stakeholders for the security consultants evaluation?
<--- Score

43. What should a proof of concept or pilot accomplish?
<--- Score

44. How are policy decisions made and where?
<--- Score

45. Are there any constraints (technical, political, cultural, or otherwise) that would inhibit certain solutions?
<--- Score

46. Is the solution technically practical?
<--- Score

47. What is the implementation plan?
<--- Score

48. What is the magnitude of the improvements?
<--- Score

49. How do you improve productivity?
<--- Score

50. How can the phases of security consultants development be identified?

<--- Score

51. Are you assessing security consultants and risk?
<--- Score

52. What is the risk?
<--- Score

53. Is supporting security consultants documentation required?
<--- Score

54. When you map the key players in your own work and the types/domains of relationships with them, which relationships do you find easy and which challenging, and why?
<--- Score

55. How can you improve performance?
<--- Score

56. How risky is your organization?
<--- Score

57. How do you improve security consultants service perception, and satisfaction?
<--- Score

58. Explorations of the frontiers of security consultants will help you build influence, improve security consultants, optimize decision making, and sustain change, what is your approach?
<--- Score

59. Is there a small-scale pilot for proposed improvement(s)? What conclusions were drawn from

the outcomes of a pilot?
<--- Score

60. Do those selected for the security consultants team have a good general understanding of what security consultants is all about?
<--- Score

61. What tools were used to evaluate the potential solutions?
<--- Score

62. Who will be responsible for making the decisions to include or exclude requested changes once security consultants is underway?
<--- Score

63. How can you improve security consultants?
<--- Score

64. Who do you report security consultants results to?
<--- Score

65. Is any security consultants documentation required?
<--- Score

66. Can the solution be designed and implemented within an acceptable time period?
<--- Score

67. Describe the design of the pilot and what tests were conducted, if any?
<--- Score

68. What were the criteria for evaluating a security consultants pilot?
<--- Score

69. What tools were most useful during the improve phase?
<--- Score

70. Why improve in the first place?
<--- Score

71. Are risk triggers captured?
<--- Score

72. Are events managed to resolution?
<--- Score

73. How do you decide how much to remunerate an employee?
<--- Score

74. Who should make the security consultants decisions?
<--- Score

75. How will the group know that the solution worked?
<--- Score

76. Risk factors: what are the characteristics of security consultants that make it risky?
<--- Score

77. How are security consultants risks managed?
<--- Score

78. Does the goal represent a desired result that can be measured?
<--- Score

79. Will the controls trigger any other risks?
<--- Score

80. Are possible solutions generated and tested?
<--- Score

81. For decision problems, how do you develop a decision statement?
<--- Score

82. Who makes the security consultants decisions in your organization?
<--- Score

83. Were any criteria developed to assist the team in testing and evaluating potential solutions?
<--- Score

84. How does the team improve its work?
<--- Score

85. Who manages security consultants risk?
<--- Score

86. Do you cover the five essential competencies: Communication, Collaboration,Innovation, Adaptability, and Leadership that improve an organizations ability to leverage the new security consultants in a volatile global economy?
<--- Score

87. Is a solution implementation plan established,

including schedule/work breakdown structure, resources, risk management plan, cost/budget, and control plan?
<--- Score

88. How do the security consultants results compare with the performance of your competitors and other organizations with similar offerings?
<--- Score

89. Is risk periodically assessed?
<--- Score

90. How do you manage and improve your security consultants work systems to deliver customer value and achieve organizational success and sustainability?
<--- Score

91. What error proofing will be done to address some of the discrepancies observed in the 'as is' process?
<--- Score

92. How do you measure improved security consultants service perception, and satisfaction?
<--- Score

93. How will you know that a change is an improvement?
<--- Score

94. What can you do to improve?
<--- Score

95. Do vendor agreements bring new compliance risk ?

<--- Score

96. Are new and improved process ('should be') maps developed?
<--- Score

97. What are the concrete security consultants results?
<--- Score

98. How does your organization evaluate strategic security consultants success?
<--- Score

99. Is the optimal solution selected based on testing and analysis?
<--- Score

100. What strategies for security consultants improvement are successful?
<--- Score

101. What resources are required for the improvement efforts?
<--- Score

102. What area needs the greatest improvement?
<--- Score

103. Which security consultants solution is appropriate?
<--- Score

104. How will you measure the results?
<--- Score

105. Is pilot data collected and analyzed?
<--- Score

106. How do you measure progress and evaluate training effectiveness?
<--- Score

107. Risk Identification: What are the possible risk events your organization faces in relation to security consultants?
<--- Score

108. What risks do you need to manage?
<--- Score

109. Is there a high likelihood that any recommendations will achieve their intended results?
<--- Score

110. Are decisions made in a timely manner?
<--- Score

111. What does the 'should be' process map/design look like?
<--- Score

112. If you could go back in time five years, what decision would you make differently? What is your best guess as to what decision you're making today you might regret five years from now?
<--- Score

113. What were the underlying assumptions on the cost-benefit analysis?
<--- Score

114. What are your current levels and trends in key measures or indicators of workforce and leader development?
<--- Score

115. How scalable is your security consultants solution?
<--- Score

116. What tools do you use once you have decided on a security consultants strategy and more importantly how do you choose?
<--- Score

117. How will you know that you have improved?
<--- Score

118. Who will be responsible for documenting the security consultants requirements in detail?
<--- Score

119. How do you go about comparing security consultants approaches/solutions?
<--- Score

120. Is the scope clearly documented?
<--- Score

121. What tools were used to tap into the creativity and encourage 'outside the box' thinking?
<--- Score

122. For estimation problems, how do you develop an estimation statement?
<--- Score

123. Is the implementation plan designed?
<--- Score

124. How do you keep improving security consultants?
<--- Score

125. What do you want to improve?
<--- Score

126. What practices helps your organization to develop its capacity to recognize patterns?
<--- Score

127. What communications are necessary to support the implementation of the solution?
<--- Score

128. How do you define the solutions' scope?
<--- Score

129. In the past few months, what is the smallest change you have made that has had the biggest positive result? What was it about that small change that produced the large return?
<--- Score

130. How will you know when its improved?
<--- Score

131. Is the measure of success for security consultants understandable to a variety of people?
<--- Score

132. How do you measure risk?

<--- Score

Add up total points for this section:
_____ = Total points for this section

Divided by: ______ (number of statements answered) = ______ Average score for this section

Transfer your score to the security consultants Index at the beginning of the Self-Assessment.

CRITERION #6: CONTROL:

INTENT: Implement the practical solution. Maintain the performance and correct possible complications.

In my belief, the answer to this question is clearly defined:

5 Strongly Agree

4 Agree

3 Neutral

2 Disagree

1 Strongly Disagree

1. How will security consultants decisions be made and monitored?
<--- Score

2. Are there documented procedures?
<--- Score

3. What are your results for key measures or indicators of the accomplishment of your security

consultants strategy and action plans, including building and strengthening core competencies?
<--- Score

4. What are customers monitoring?
<--- Score

5. Is a response plan in place for when the input, process, or output measures indicate an 'out-of-control' condition?
<--- Score

6. Do you monitor the security consultants decisions made and fine tune them as they evolve?
<--- Score

7. Are the security consultants standards challenging?
<--- Score

8. How do you encourage people to take control and responsibility?
<--- Score

9. What are you attempting to measure/monitor?
<--- Score

10. How will new or emerging customer needs/requirements be checked/communicated to orient the process toward meeting the new specifications and continually reducing variation?
<--- Score

11. Is there a standardized process?
<--- Score

12. How can you best use all of your knowledge repositories to enhance learning and sharing?
<--- Score

13. In the case of a security consultants project, the criteria for the audit derive from implementation objectives, an audit of a security consultants project involves assessing whether the recommendations outlined for implementation have been met, can you track that any security consultants project is implemented as planned, and is it working?
<--- Score

14. Who has control over resources?
<--- Score

15. Are pertinent alerts monitored, analyzed and distributed to appropriate personnel?
<--- Score

16. Implementation Planning: is a pilot needed to test the changes before a full roll out occurs?
<--- Score

17. Is there a control plan in place for sustaining improvements (short and long-term)?
<--- Score

18. How will the day-to-day responsibilities for monitoring and continual improvement be transferred from the improvement team to the process owner?
<--- Score

19. Is there a transfer of ownership and knowledge

to process owner and process team tasked with the responsibilities.
<--- Score

20. How will input, process, and output variables be checked to detect for sub-optimal conditions?
<--- Score

21. Who will be in control?
<--- Score

22. Is reporting being used or needed?
<--- Score

23. Is knowledge gained on process shared and institutionalized?
<--- Score

24. How widespread is its use?
<--- Score

25. Is a response plan established and deployed?
<--- Score

26. What is the control/monitoring plan?
<--- Score

27. What adjustments to the strategies are needed?
<--- Score

28. Are new process steps, standards, and documentation ingrained into normal operations?
<--- Score

29. Is there a recommended audit plan for routine

surveillance inspections of security consultants's gains?
<--- Score

30. What is the standard for acceptable security consultants performance?
<--- Score

31. What is your theory of human motivation, and how does your compensation plan fit with that view?
<--- Score

32. Are the planned controls working?
<--- Score

33. What are the key elements of your security consultants performance improvement system, including your evaluation, organizational learning, and innovation processes?
<--- Score

34. How likely is the current security consultants plan to come in on schedule or on budget?
<--- Score

35. What is the best design framework for security consultants organization now that, in a post industrial-age if the top-down, command and control model is no longer relevant?
<--- Score

36. Is new knowledge gained imbedded in the response plan?
<--- Score

37. Are you measuring, monitoring and predicting

security consultants activities to optimize operations and profitability, and enhancing outcomes?
<--- Score

38. What is the recommended frequency of auditing?
<--- Score

39. Will any special training be provided for results interpretation?
<--- Score

40. What quality tools were useful in the control phase?
<--- Score

41. What is your plan to assess your security risks?
<--- Score

42. Will your goals reflect your program budget?
<--- Score

43. What do you stand for--and what are you against?
<--- Score

44. How will you measure your QA plan's effectiveness?
<--- Score

45. Is there documentation that will support the successful operation of the improvement?
<--- Score

46. Will the team be available to assist members in planning investigations?
<--- Score

47. What do your reports reflect?
<--- Score

48. How will report readings be checked to effectively monitor performance?
<--- Score

49. How do senior leaders actions reflect a commitment to the organizations security consultants values?
<--- Score

50. Are the planned controls in place?
<--- Score

51. How do your controls stack up?
<--- Score

52. What other areas of the group might benefit from the security consultants team's improvements, knowledge, and learning?
<--- Score

53. Against what alternative is success being measured?
<--- Score

54. How do you plan on providing proper recognition and disclosure of supporting companies?
<--- Score

55. What are the critical parameters to watch?
<--- Score

56. Do you monitor the effectiveness of your security consultants activities?

<--- Score

57. How do you spread information?
<--- Score

58. How do you select, collect, align, and integrate security consultants data and information for tracking daily operations and overall organizational performance, including progress relative to strategic objectives and action plans?
<--- Score

59. What should the next improvement project be that is related to security consultants?
<--- Score

60. Have new or revised work instructions resulted?
<--- Score

61. What other systems, operations, processes, and infrastructures (hiring practices, staffing, training, incentives/rewards, metrics/dashboards/scorecards, etc.) need updates, additions, changes, or deletions in order to facilitate knowledge transfer and improvements?
<--- Score

62. Do the security consultants decisions you make today help people and the planet tomorrow?
<--- Score

63. How do controls support value?
<--- Score

64. Are controls in place and consistently applied?
<--- Score

65. Who sets the security consultants standards?
<--- Score

66. How do you monitor usage and cost?
<--- Score

67. Who is going to spread your message?
<--- Score

68. How do you plan for the cost of succession?
<--- Score

69. Who is the security consultants process owner?
<--- Score

70. How is security consultants project cost planned, managed, monitored?
<--- Score

71. What should you measure to verify efficiency gains?
<--- Score

72. How do you establish and deploy modified action plans if circumstances require a shift in plans and rapid execution of new plans?
<--- Score

73. Where do ideas that reach policy makers and planners as proposals for security consultants strengthening and reform actually originate?
<--- Score

74. How is change control managed?
<--- Score

75. Can you adapt and adjust to changing security consultants situations?
<--- Score

76. Has the security consultants value of standards been quantified?
<--- Score

77. Can support from partners be adjusted?
<--- Score

78. Is there a documented and implemented monitoring plan?
<--- Score

79. Are suggested corrective/restorative actions indicated on the response plan for known causes to problems that might surface?
<--- Score

80. You may have created your quality measures at a time when you lacked resources, technology wasn't up to the required standard, or low service levels were the industry norm. Have those circumstances changed?
<--- Score

81. How will the process owner verify improvement in present and future sigma levels, process capabilities?
<--- Score

82. Who controls critical resources?
<--- Score

83. Will existing staff require re-training, for example,

to learn new business processes?
<--- Score

84. Does the security consultants performance meet the customer's requirements?
<--- Score

85. How will the process owner and team be able to hold the gains?
<--- Score

86. What key inputs and outputs are being measured on an ongoing basis?
<--- Score

87. Does a troubleshooting guide exist or is it needed?
<--- Score

88. What security consultants standards are applicable?
<--- Score

89. What do you measure to verify effectiveness gains?
<--- Score

90. Does job training on the documented procedures need to be part of the process team's education and training?
<--- Score

91. Does the response plan contain a definite closed loop continual improvement scheme (e.g., plan-do-check-act)?
<--- Score

92. Are operating procedures consistent?
<--- Score

93. How might the group capture best practices and lessons learned so as to leverage improvements?
<--- Score

94. Are documented procedures clear and easy to follow for the operators?
<--- Score

95. Has the improved process and its steps been standardized?
<--- Score

96. Is there an action plan in case of emergencies?
<--- Score

Add up total points for this section:
_____ = Total points for this section

Divided by: ______ (number of statements answered) = ______ Average score for this section

Transfer your score to the security consultants Index at the beginning of the Self-Assessment.

CRITERION #7: SUSTAIN:

INTENT: Retain the benefits.

In my belief, the answer to this question is clearly defined:

5 Strongly Agree

4 Agree

3 Neutral

2 Disagree

1 Strongly Disagree

1. In retrospect, of the projects that you pulled the plug on, what percent do you wish had been allowed to keep going, and what percent do you wish had ended earlier?
<--- Score

2. Do you have an implicit bias for capital investments over people investments?
<--- Score

3. How likely is it that a customer would recommend

your company to a friend or colleague?
<--- Score

4. Whose voice (department, ethnic group, women, older workers, etc) might you have missed hearing from in your company, and how might you amplify this voice to create positive momentum for your business?
<--- Score

5. What are the performance and scale of the security consultants tools?
<--- Score

6. Is security consultants realistic, or are you setting yourself up for failure?
<--- Score

7. Are new benefits received and understood?
<--- Score

8. Why should you adopt a security consultants framework?
<--- Score

9. How do you make it meaningful in connecting security consultants with what users do day-to-day?
<--- Score

10. How important is security consultants to the user organizations mission?
<--- Score

11. Do you know what you are doing? And who do you call if you don't?
<--- Score

12. What potential megatrends could make your business model obsolete?
<--- Score

13. If you find that you havent accomplished one of the goals for one of the steps of the security consultants strategy, what will you do to fix it?
<--- Score

14. What security consultants skills are most important?
<--- Score

15. Which security consultants goals are the most important?
<--- Score

16. What are your most important goals for the strategic security consultants objectives?
<--- Score

17. What counts that you are not counting?
<--- Score

18. What information is critical to your organization that your executives are ignoring?
<--- Score

19. What is your question? Why?
<--- Score

20. Are all key stakeholders present at all Structured Walkthroughs?
<--- Score

21. How do you maintain security consultants's Integrity?
<--- Score

22. How can you become the company that would put you out of business?
<--- Score

23. What is the craziest thing you can do?
<--- Score

24. What would you recommend your friend do if he/she were facing this dilemma?
<--- Score

25. Is a security consultants team work effort in place?
<--- Score

26. How do you cross-sell and up-sell your security consultants success?
<--- Score

27. Why is it important to have senior management support for a security consultants project?
<--- Score

28. What is it like to work for you?
<--- Score

29. Who is the main stakeholder, with ultimate responsibility for driving security consultants forward?
<--- Score

30. What are the key enablers to make this security consultants move?

<--- Score

31. How much does security consultants help?
<--- Score

32. Can the schedule be done in the given time?
<--- Score

33. How can you become more high-tech but still be high touch?
<--- Score

34. Can you break it down?
<--- Score

35. What are you challenging?
<--- Score

36. How do you set security consultants stretch targets and how do you get people to not only participate in setting these stretch targets but also that they strive to achieve these?
<--- Score

37. Which functions and people interact with the supplier and or customer?
<--- Score

38. If there were zero limitations, what would you do differently?
<--- Score

39. What are current security consultants paradigms?
<--- Score

40. What is the purpose of security consultants in

relation to the mission?
<--- Score

41. Who are the key stakeholders?
<--- Score

42. Think of your security consultants project, what are the main functions?
<--- Score

43. Who will provide the final approval of security consultants deliverables?
<--- Score

44. Why is security consultants important for you now?
<--- Score

45. Who uses your product in ways you never expected?
<--- Score

46. What are the short and long-term security consultants goals?
<--- Score

47. What are the usability implications of security consultants actions?
<--- Score

48. Are you / should you be revolutionary or evolutionary?
<--- Score

49. What knowledge, skills and characteristics mark a good security consultants project manager?

<--- Score

50. Did your employees make progress today?
<--- Score

51. How long will it take to change?
<--- Score

52. What trouble can you get into?
<--- Score

53. How do you determine the key elements that affect security consultants workforce satisfaction, how are these elements determined for different workforce groups and segments?
<--- Score

54. What are specific security consultants rules to follow?
<--- Score

55. How do you create buy-in?
<--- Score

56. In a project to restructure security consultants outcomes, which stakeholders would you involve?
<--- Score

57. How do you ensure that implementations of security consultants products are done in a way that ensures safety?
<--- Score

58. Operational - will it work?
<--- Score

59. What new services of functionality will be implemented next with security consultants ?
<--- Score

60. What is the source of the strategies for security consultants strengthening and reform?
<--- Score

61. Is the impact that security consultants has shown?
<--- Score

62. Can you do all this work?
<--- Score

63. Is there a work around that you can use?
<--- Score

64. How much contingency will be available in the budget?
<--- Score

65. What is your BATNA (best alternative to a negotiated agreement)?
<--- Score

66. What is effective security consultants?
<--- Score

67. Do you think you know, or do you know you know ?
<--- Score

68. Is there any existing security consultants governance structure?
<--- Score

69. If you do not follow, then how to lead?
<--- Score

70. Do you say no to customers for no reason?
<--- Score

71. Who are your customers?
<--- Score

72. Who do we want your customers to become?
<--- Score

73. What are internal and external security consultants relations?
<--- Score

74. Has implementation been effective in reaching specified objectives so far?
<--- Score

75. Is there any reason to believe the opposite of my current belief?
<--- Score

76. What could happen if you do not do it?
<--- Score

77. What are the essentials of internal security consultants management?
<--- Score

78. How will you motivate the stakeholders with the least vested interest?
<--- Score

79. Do you see more potential in people than they do

in themselves?
<--- Score

80. Have new benefits been realized?
<--- Score

81. Is your strategy driving your strategy? Or is the way in which you allocate resources driving your strategy?
<--- Score

82. What is the kind of project structure that would be appropriate for your security consultants project, should it be formal and complex, or can it be less formal and relatively simple?
<--- Score

83. What do we do when new problems arise?
<--- Score

84. Who, on the executive team or the board, has spoken to a customer recently?
<--- Score

85. Is your basic point _____ or _____?
<--- Score

86. Who will determine interim and final deadlines?
<--- Score

87. What is the funding source for this project?
<--- Score

88. How do you keep the momentum going?
<--- Score

89. What are the potential basics of security consultants fraud?
<--- Score

90. What security consultants modifications can you make work for you?
<--- Score

91. Which models, tools and techniques are necessary?
<--- Score

92. What have you done to protect your business from competitive encroachment?
<--- Score

93. How do you assess the security consultants pitfalls that are inherent in implementing it?
<--- Score

94. What is something you believe that nearly no one agrees with you on?
<--- Score

95. What happens when a new employee joins the organization?
<--- Score

96. Are the assumptions believable and achievable?
<--- Score

97. Is security consultants dependent on the successful delivery of a current project?
<--- Score

98. To whom do you add value?
<--- Score

99. If no one would ever find out about your accomplishments, how would you lead differently?
<--- Score

100. What trophy do you want on your mantle?
<--- Score

101. Who do you want your customers to become?
<--- Score

102. Do you have past security consultants successes?
<--- Score

103. Where can you break convention?
<--- Score

104. If you got fired and a new hire took your place, what would she do different?
<--- Score

105. What are the challenges?
<--- Score

106. What is your security consultants strategy?
<--- Score

107. When information truly is ubiquitous, when reach and connectivity are completely global, when computing resources are infinite, and when a whole new set of impossibilities are not only possible, but happening, what will that do to your business?
<--- Score

108. What does your signature ensure?
<--- Score

109. What should you stop doing?
<--- Score

110. Who else should you help?
<--- Score

111. Instead of going to current contacts for new ideas, what if you reconnected with dormant contacts--the people you used to know? If you were going reactivate a dormant tie, who would it be?
<--- Score

112. If your company went out of business tomorrow, would anyone who doesn't get a paycheck here care?
<--- Score

113. If you had to leave your organization for a year and the only communication you could have with employees/colleagues was a single paragraph, what would you write?
<--- Score

114. Do you think security consultants accomplishes the goals you expect it to accomplish?
<--- Score

115. Who have you, as a company, historically been when you've been at your best?
<--- Score

116. How will you insure seamless interoperability

of security consultants moving forward?
<--- Score

117. Do security consultants rules make a reasonable demand on a users capabilities?
<--- Score

118. Who will be responsible for deciding whether security consultants goes ahead or not after the initial investigations?
<--- Score

119. What are the success criteria that will indicate that security consultants objectives have been met and the benefits delivered?
<--- Score

120. How do you manage security consultants Knowledge Management (KM)?
<--- Score

121. How does security consultants integrate with other stakeholder initiatives?
<--- Score

122. How will you know that the security consultants project has been successful?
<--- Score

123. Why should people listen to you?
<--- Score

124. Is the security consultants organization completing tasks effectively and efficiently?
<--- Score

125. Are you making progress, and are you making progress as security consultants leaders?
<--- Score

126. How can you incorporate support to ensure safe and effective use of security consultants into the services that you provide?
<--- Score

127. How do you deal with security consultants changes?
<--- Score

128. What is your competitive advantage?
<--- Score

129. What you are going to do to affect the numbers?
<--- Score

130. How are you doing compared to your industry?
<--- Score

131. What is the big security consultants idea?
<--- Score

132. What relationships among security consultants trends do you perceive?
<--- Score

133. Are you changing as fast as the world around you?
<--- Score

134. Have benefits been optimized with all key stakeholders?

<--- Score

135. What business benefits will security consultants goals deliver if achieved?
<--- Score

136. Who are four people whose careers you have enhanced?
<--- Score

137. What is a feasible sequencing of reform initiatives over time?
<--- Score

138. If you had to rebuild your organization without any traditional competitive advantages (i.e., no killer technology, promising research, innovative product/service delivery model, etcetera), how would your people have to approach their work and collaborate together in order to create the necessary conditions for success?
<--- Score

139. Whom among your colleagues do you trust, and for what?
<--- Score

140. Were lessons learned captured and communicated?
<--- Score

141. Is a security consultants breakthrough on the horizon?
<--- Score

142. How do you foster innovation?

<--- Score

143. What goals did you miss?
<--- Score

144. Will it be accepted by users?
<--- Score

145. What management system can you use to leverage the security consultants experience, ideas, and concerns of the people closest to the work to be done?
<--- Score

146. Would you rather sell to knowledgeable and informed customers or to uninformed customers?
<--- Score

147. How do you track customer value, profitability or financial return, organizational success, and sustainability?
<--- Score

148. What are the long-term security consultants goals?
<--- Score

149. What is the recommended frequency of auditing?
<--- Score

150. Political -is anyone trying to undermine this project?
<--- Score

151. Are there any activities that you can take off your to do list?

<--- Score

152. If your customer were your grandmother, would you tell her to buy what you're selling?
<--- Score

153. What current systems have to be understood and/or changed?
<--- Score

154. Are the criteria for selecting recommendations stated?
<--- Score

155. Who do you think the world wants your organization to be?
<--- Score

156. How do senior leaders deploy your organizations vision and values through your leadership system, to the workforce, to key suppliers and partners, and to customers and other stakeholders, as appropriate?
<--- Score

157. How do you proactively clarify deliverables and security consultants quality expectations?
<--- Score

158. How do you transition from the baseline to the target?
<--- Score

159. What was the last experiment you ran?
<--- Score

160. Can you maintain your growth without detracting from the factors that have contributed to your success?
<--- Score

161. What is an unauthorized commitment?
<--- Score

162. What are the top 3 things at the forefront of your security consultants agendas for the next 3 years?
<--- Score

163. Is maximizing security consultants protection the same as minimizing security consultants loss?
<--- Score

164. Who will manage the integration of tools?
<--- Score

165. How do you foster the skills, knowledge, talents, attributes, and characteristics you want to have?
<--- Score

166. What are the rules and assumptions your industry operates under? What if the opposite were true?
<--- Score

167. What are the gaps in your knowledge and experience?
<--- Score

168. How do you engage the workforce, in addition to satisfying them?
<--- Score

169. What are the barriers to increased security consultants production?
<--- Score

170. What is your formula for success in security consultants ?
<--- Score

171. Why not do security consultants?
<--- Score

172. Why do and why don't your customers like your organization?
<--- Score

173. Why will customers want to buy your organizations products/services?
<--- Score

174. What would have to be true for the option on the table to be the best possible choice?
<--- Score

175. How can you negotiate security consultants successfully with a stubborn boss, an irate client, or a deceitful coworker?
<--- Score

176. How do you know if you are successful?
<--- Score

177. How do you go about securing security consultants?
<--- Score

178. How will you ensure you get what you

expected?
<--- Score

179. Are you using a design thinking approach and integrating Innovation, security consultants Experience, and Brand Value?
<--- Score

180. How do you accomplish your long range security consultants goals?
<--- Score

181. What must you excel at?
<--- Score

182. What are strategies for increasing support and reducing opposition?
<--- Score

183. What happens at your organization when people fail?
<--- Score

184. Who is responsible for ensuring appropriate resources (time, people and money) are allocated to security consultants?
<--- Score

185. Do you feel that more should be done in the security consultants area?
<--- Score

186. What are your personal philosophies regarding security consultants and how do they influence your work?
<--- Score

187. How do you stay inspired?
<--- Score

188. Do you know who is a friend or a foe?
<--- Score

189. At what moment would you think; Will I get fired?
<--- Score

190. How do you lead with security consultants in mind?
<--- Score

191. What role does communication play in the success or failure of a security consultants project?
<--- Score

192. Is it economical; do you have the time and money?
<--- Score

193. Which individuals, teams or departments will be involved in security consultants?
<--- Score

194. What are the business goals security consultants is aiming to achieve?
<--- Score

195. Are you satisfied with your current role? If not, what is missing from it?
<--- Score

196. How do you provide a safe environment -physically and emotionally?

<--- Score

197. How do you listen to customers to obtain actionable information?
<--- Score

198. How is implementation research currently incorporated into each of your goals?
<--- Score

199. Do you have the right people on the bus?
<--- Score

200. If you were responsible for initiating and implementing major changes in your organization, what steps might you take to ensure acceptance of those changes?
<--- Score

201. Are you maintaining a past–present–future perspective throughout the security consultants discussion?
<--- Score

202. What may be the consequences for the performance of an organization if all stakeholders are not consulted regarding security consultants?
<--- Score

203. Marketing budgets are tighter, consumers are more skeptical, and social media has changed forever the way we talk about security consultants, how do you gain traction?
<--- Score

204. How do you keep records, of what?

<--- Score

205. In the past year, what have you done (or could you have done) to increase the accurate perception of your company/brand as ethical and honest?
<--- Score

206. How do you govern and fulfill your societal responsibilities?
<--- Score

207. What is the range of capabilities?
<--- Score

208. What happens if you do not have enough funding?
<--- Score

209. What will be the consequences to the stakeholder (financial, reputation etc) if security consultants does not go ahead or fails to deliver the objectives?
<--- Score

210. What threat is security consultants addressing?
<--- Score

211. Will there be any necessary staff changes (redundancies or new hires)?
<--- Score

212. What is the overall talent health of your organization as a whole at senior levels, and for each organization reporting to a member of the Senior Leadership Team?
<--- Score

213. Who is responsible for security consultants?
<--- Score

214. If you weren't already in this business, would you enter it today? And if not, what are you going to do about it?
<--- Score

215. Who is responsible for errors?
<--- Score

216. What stupid rule would you most like to kill?
<--- Score

217. What did you miss in the interview for the worst hire you ever made?
<--- Score

218. How do customers see your organization?
<--- Score

219. What is the estimated value of the project?
<--- Score

220. What are you trying to prove to yourself, and how might it be hijacking your life and business success?
<--- Score

221. Are your responses positive or negative?
<--- Score

Add up total points for this section:
_____ = Total points for this section

Divided by: ______ (number of

statements answered) = ______
Average score for this section

Transfer your score to the security consultants Index at the beginning of the Self-Assessment.

Security Consultants and Managing Projects, Criteria for Project Managers:

1.0 Initiating Process Group: Security Consultants

1. What business situation is being addressed?

2. Are there resources to maintain and support the outcome of the Security Consultants project?

3. Did the Security Consultants project team have the right skills?

4. Do you know if the Security Consultants project requires outside equipment or vendor resources?

5. Do you understand the quality and control criteria that must be achieved for successful Security Consultants project completion?

6. Professionals want to know what is expected from them what are the deliverables?

7. How should needs be met?

8. Based on your Security Consultants project communication management plan, what worked well?

9. Do you know the roles & responsibilities required for this Security Consultants project?

10. Were resources available as planned?

11. How will it affect me?

12. How do you help others satisfy needs?

13. What are the inputs required to produce the deliverables?

14. Are you properly tracking the progress of the Security Consultants project and communicating the status to stakeholders?

15. Information sharing?

16. During which stage of Risk planning are modeling techniques used to determine overall effects of risks on Security Consultants project objectives for high probability, high impact risks?

17. Were decisions made in a timely manner?

18. The Security Consultants project you are managing has nine stakeholders. How many channel of communications are there between corresponding stakeholders?

19. Do you know the Security Consultants projects goal, purpose and objectives?

20. Who are the Security Consultants project stakeholders?

1.1 Project Charter: Security Consultants

21. Why do you manage integration?

22. How do you manage integration?

23. What is the business need?

24. What ideas do you have for initial tests of change (PDSA cycles)?

25. How will you know that a change is an improvement?

26. Customer benefits: what customer requirements does this Security Consultants project address?

27. Why have you chosen the aim you have set forth?

28. What are the constraints?

29. Security Consultants project objective statement: what must the Security Consultants project do?

30. What are you striving to accomplish (measurable goal(s))?

31. What is the purpose of the Security Consultants project?

32. Why the improvements?

33. What is the most common tool for helping define the detail?

34. Customer: who are you doing the Security Consultants project for?

35. Review the general mission What system will be affected by the improvement efforts?

36. Where and how does the team fit within your organization structure?

37. What date will the task finish?

38. Did your Security Consultants project ask for this?

39. Why is it important?

40. Who ise input and support will this Security Consultants project require?

1.2 Stakeholder Register: Security Consultants

41. What are the major Security Consultants project milestones requiring communications or providing communications opportunities?

42. What & Why?

43. How should employers make voices heard?

44. Who is managing stakeholder engagement?

45. How will reports be created?

46. What opportunities exist to provide communications?

47. How big is the gap?

48. Who are the stakeholders?

49. Who wants to talk about Security?

50. How much influence do they have on the Security Consultants project?

51. What is the power of the stakeholder?

52. Is your organization ready for change?

1.3 Stakeholder Analysis Matrix: Security Consultants

53. Are you going to weigh the stakeholders?

54. Who influences whom?

55. Who will be affected by the work?

56. Philosophy and values?

57. Why is it important to identify them?

58. Participatory approach: how will key stakeholders participate in the Security Consultants project?

59. Why do you need to manage Security Consultants project Risk?

60. Is there a reason why you are or are not not using an external rating system?

61. What organizational arrangements are planned to ensure the Security Consultants project achieves its social development outcomes?

62. Who is most dependent on the resources at stake?

63. Who will promote/support the Security Consultants project, provided that they are involved?

64. What coalitions might build around the issues being tackled?

65. What is your Advocacy Strategy?

66. Accreditations, etc?

67. What are the opportunities for communication?

68. Cashflow, start-up cash-drain?

69. Guiding question: who shall you involve in the making of the stakeholder map?

70. Opponents; who are the opponents?

71. Arena: in what fields are the actors active, where are they present?

72. Processes and systems, etc?

2.0 Planning Process Group: Security Consultants

73. If action is called for, what form should it take?

74. Explanation: is what the Security Consultants project intents to solve a hard question?

75. How are the principles of aid effectiveness (ownership, alignment, management for development results and mutual responsibility) being applied in the Security Consultants project?

76. Have operating capacities been created and/or reinforced in partners?

77. Who are the Security Consultants project stakeholders?

78. In what way has the Security Consultants project come up with innovative measures for problem-solving?

79. How well do the team follow the chosen processes?

80. If a risk event occurs, what will you do?

81. How can you make your needs known?

82. Do the partners have sufficient financial capacity to keep up the benefits produced by the programme?

83. Are the necessary foundations in place to ensure the sustainability of the results of the Security Consultants project?

84. First of all, should any action be taken?

85. What is the NEXT thing to do?

86. What do you need to do?

87. Are the follow-up indicators relevant and do they meet the quality needed to measure the outputs and outcomes of the Security Consultants project?

88. Is the Security Consultants project making progress in helping to achieve the set results?

89. Does it make any difference if you are successful?

90. Did you read it correctly?

91. If task x starts two days late, what is the effect on the Security Consultants project end date?

92. How do you integrate Security Consultants project Planning with the Iterative/Evolutionary SDLC?

2.1 Project Management Plan: Security Consultants

93. What does management expect of PMs?

94. What is risk management?

95. Are alternatives safe, functional, constructible, economical, reasonable and sustainable?

96. Do the proposed changes from the Security Consultants project include any significant risks to safety?

97. What are the training needs?

98. Who manages integration?

99. When is a Security Consultants project management plan created?

100. Did the planning effort collaborate to develop solutions that integrate expertise, policies, programs, and Security Consultants projects across entities?

101. Where does all this information come from?

102. What went right?

103. Who is the Security Consultants project Manager?

104. Does the selected plan protect privacy?

105. What is the justification?

106. Is the appropriate plan selected based on your organizations objectives and evaluation criteria expressed in Principles and Guidelines policies?

107. What if, for example, the positive direction and vision of your organization causes expected trends to change resulting in greater need than expected?

108. Who is the sponsor?

109. What are the assumptions?

110. Are there any windfall benefits that would accrue to the Security Consultants project sponsor or other parties?

2.2 Scope Management Plan: Security Consultants

111. Is there a Steering Committee in place?

112. What work performance data will be captured?

113. Are you doing what you have set out to do?

114. Is there an issues management plan in place?

115. Has the Security Consultants project manager been identified?

116. Are the results of quality assurance reviews provided to affected groups & individuals?

117. Is the steering committee active in Security Consultants project oversight?

118. Is there an onboarding process in place?

119. Are you spending the right amount of money for specific tasks?

120. Where do scope processes fit in?

121. Is stakeholder involvement adequate?

122. Has the budget been baselined?

123. Are multiple estimation methods being employed?

124. Are issues raised, assessed, actioned, and resolved in a timely and efficient manner?

125. Timeline and milestones?

126. Have the scope, objectives, costs, benefits and impacts been communicated to all involved and/or impacted stakeholders and work groups?

127. Is there any form of automated support for Issues Management?

128. Deliverables -are the deliverables tangible and verifiable?

129. Are decisions captured in a decisions log?

130. Function of the configuration control board?

2.3 Requirements Management Plan: Security Consultants

131. Is stakeholder risk tolerance an important factor for the requirements process in this Security Consultants project?

132. Which hardware or software, related to, or as outcome of the Security Consultants project is new to your organization?

133. Does the Security Consultants project have a Change Control process?

134. Did you provide clear and concise specifications?

135. Why manage requirements?

136. Are actual resources expenditures versus planned expenditures acceptable?

137. Are all the stakeholders ready for the transition into the user community?

138. Who will finally present the work or product(s) for acceptance?

139. Do you really need to write this document at all?

140. Do you know which stakeholders will participate in the requirements effort?

141. Do you understand the role that each

stakeholder will play in the requirements process?

142. Have stakeholders been instructed in the Change Control process?

143. What cost metrics will be used?

144. What information regarding the Security Consultants project requirements will be reported?

145. What is the earliest finish date for this Security Consultants project if it is scheduled to start on ...?

146. Do you expect stakeholders to be cooperative?

147. Could inaccurate or incomplete requirements in this Security Consultants project create a serious risk for the business?

148. Who is responsible for monitoring and tracking the Security Consultants project requirements?

149. Describe the process for rejecting the Security Consultants project requirements. Who has the authority to reject Security Consultants project requirements?

150. What are you counting on?

2.4 Requirements Documentation: Security Consultants

151. Who is interacting with the system?

152. What happens when requirements are wrong?

153. Basic work/business process; high-level, what is being touched?

154. What can tools do for us?

155. How will the proposed Security Consultants project help?

156. How much does requirements engineering cost?

157. How can you document system requirements?

158. What will be the integration problems?

159. Can the requirements be checked?

160. Who is involved?

161. Are all functions required by the customer included?

162. How linear / iterative is your Requirements Gathering process (or will it be)?

163. Who provides requirements?

164. Where do you define what is a customer, what are the attributes of customer?

165. Does the system provide the functions which best support the customers needs?

166. Has requirements gathering uncovered information that would necessitate changes?

167. Is the origin of the requirement clearly stated?

168. The problem with gathering requirements is right there in the word gathering. What images does it conjure?

169. What is effective documentation?

170. Is new technology needed?

2.5 Requirements Traceability Matrix: Security Consultants

171. Do you have a clear understanding of all subcontracts in place?

172. What are the chronologies, contingencies, consequences, criteria?

173. Is there a requirements traceability process in place?

174. What is the WBS?

175. How small is small enough?

176. Describe the process for approving requirements so they can be added to the traceability matrix and Security Consultants project work can be performed. Will the Security Consultants project requirements become approved in writing?

177. Will you use a Requirements Traceability Matrix?

178. How do you manage scope?

179. Why do you manage scope?

180. How will it affect the stakeholders personally in career?

181. Why use a WBS?

182. What percentage of Security Consultants projects are producing traceability matrices between requirements and other work products?

2.6 Project Scope Statement: Security Consultants

183. Elements of scope management that deal with concept development ?

184. Are there specific processes you will use to evaluate and approve/reject changes?

185. Is the plan for Security Consultants project resources adequate?

186. Will the qa related information be reported regularly as part of the status reporting mechanisms?

187. Will there be a Change Control Process in place?

188. Has the format for tracking and monitoring schedules and costs been defined?

189. Will the risk documents be filed?

190. What are the defined meeting materials?

191. Is the Security Consultants project manager qualified and experienced in Security Consultants project management?

192. Have the reports to be produced, distributed, and filed been defined?

193. Is your organization structure appropriate for the Security Consultants projects size and complexity?

194. Is there an information system for the Security Consultants project?

195. Elements that deal with providing the detail?

196. What went wrong?

197. Were key Security Consultants project stakeholders brought into the Security Consultants project Plan?

198. Once its defined, what is the stability of the Security Consultants project scope?

199. Will tasks be marked complete only after QA has been successfully completed?

2.7 Assumption and Constraint Log: Security Consultants

200. Is this process still needed?

201. Are formal code reviews conducted?

202. What weaknesses do you have?

203. Has the approach and development strategy of the Security Consultants project been defined, documented and accepted by the appropriate stakeholders?

204. Is this model reasonable?

205. Are there cosmetic errors that hinder readability and comprehension?

206. Do the requirements meet the standards of correctness, completeness, consistency, accuracy, and readability?

207. What do you log?

208. Does the document/deliverable meet all requirements (for example, statement of work) specific to this deliverable?

209. Contradictory information between different documents?

210. Are there processes defining how software will

be developed including development methods, overall timeline for development, software product standards, and traceability?

211. What strengths do you have?

212. Are requirements management tracking tools and procedures in place?

213. Does the Security Consultants project have a formal Security Consultants project Plan?

214. Can the requirements be traced to the appropriate components of the solution, as well as test scripts?

215. Does the document/deliverable meet general requirements (for example, statement of work) for all deliverables?

216. Have all involved stakeholders and work groups committed to the Security Consultants project?

217. Are funding and staffing resource estimates sufficiently detailed and documented for use in planning and tracking the Security Consultants project?

2.8 Work Breakdown Structure: Security Consultants

218. When does it have to be done?

219. How will you and your Security Consultants project team define the Security Consultants projects scope and work breakdown structure?

220. Who has to do it?

221. What is the probability that the Security Consultants project duration will exceed xx weeks?

222. Where does it take place?

223. What has to be done?

224. How big is a work-package?

225. When would you develop a Work Breakdown Structure?

226. Why would you develop a Work Breakdown Structure?

227. Is it still viable?

228. What is the probability of completing the Security Consultants project in less that xx days?

229. Can you make it?

230. When do you stop?

231. How far down?

232. Is it a change in scope?

233. Why is it useful?

234. Do you need another level?

2.9 WBS Dictionary: Security Consultants

235. Are material costs reported within the same period as that in which BCWP is earned for that material?

236. Is budgeted cost for work performed calculated in a manner consistent with the way work is planned?

237. Does the contractors system provide unit or lot costs when applicable?

238. Is all contract work included in the CWBS?

239. Are the rates for allocating costs from each indirect cost pool to contracts updated as necessary to ensure a realistic monthly allocation of indirect costs without significant year-end adjustments?

240. Are records maintained to show how undistributed budgets are controlled?

241. Are current budgets resulting from changes to the authorized work and/or internal replanning, reconcilable to original budgets for specified reporting items?

242. Are data elements summarized through the functional organizational structure for progressively higher levels of management?

243. Major functional areas of contract effort?

244. Evaluate the performance of operating organizations?

245. Budgeted cost for work performed?

246. Are estimates of costs at completion generated in a rational, consistent manner?

247. Should you include sub-activities?

248. Are estimates of costs at completion utilized in determining contract funding requirements and reporting them?

249. Changes in the nature of the overhead requirements?

250. Are detailed work packages planned as far in advance as practicable?

251. Are the latest revised estimates of costs at completion compared with the established budgets at appropriate levels and causes of variances identified?

252. Is future work which cannot be planned in detail subdivided to the extent practicable for budgeting and scheduling purposes?

253. Does the cost accumulation system provide for summarization of indirect costs from the point of allocation to the contract total?

254. Are the bases and rates for allocating costs from each indirect pool to commercial work consistent with

the already stated used to allocate corresponding costs to Government contracts?

2.10 Schedule Management Plan: Security Consultants

255. Are there any activities or deliverables being added or gold-plated that could be dropped or scaled back without falling short of the original requirement?

256. Have external dependencies been captured in the schedule?

257. Are enough systems & user personnel assigned to the Security Consultants project?

258. Can be realistically shortened (the duration of subsequent tasks)?

259. How does the proposed individual meet each requirement?

260. Are the Security Consultants project team members located locally to the users/stakeholders?

261. Have reserves been created to address risks?

262. Where is the scheduling tool and who has access to it to view it?

263. Have the key functions and capabilities been defined and assigned to each release or iteration?

264. Are estimating assumptions and constraints captured?

265. Are all activities captured and do they address all approved work scope in the Security Consultants project baseline?

266. Are the key elements of a Security Consultants project Charter present?

267. Has your organization readiness assessment been conducted?

268. Identify the amount of schedule variation that triggers a warning. What happens if a warning is triggered?

269. Is your organization certified as a supplier, wholesaler and/or regular dealer?

270. Is there a procedure for management, control and release of schedule margin?

271. Has a provision been made to reassess Security Consultants project risks at various Security Consultants project stages?

2.11 Activity List: Security Consultants

272. How do you determine the late start (LS) for each activity?

273. How detailed should a Security Consultants project get?

274. What did not go as well?

275. Can you determine the activity that must finish, before this activity can start?

276. How can the Security Consultants project be displayed graphically to better visualize the activities?

277. What will be performed?

278. Is there anything planned that does not need to be here?

279. How difficult will it be to do specific activities on this Security Consultants project?

280. What are the critical bottleneck activities?

281. When do the individual activities need to start and finish?

282. What is the LF and LS for each activity?

283. Are the required resources available or need to

be acquired?

284. What is your organizations history in doing similar activities?

285. Who will perform the work?

286. What is the probability the Security Consultants project can be completed in xx weeks?

287. The wbs is developed as part of a joint planning session. and how do you know that youhave done this right?

288. For other activities, how much delay can be tolerated?

2.12 Activity Attributes: Security Consultants

289. Can more resources be added?

290. Is there a trend during the year?

291. Where else does it apply?

292. Are the required resources available?

293. How many days do you need to complete the work scope with a limit of X number of resources?

294. Were there other ways you could have organized the data to achieve similar results?

295. Would you consider either of corresponding activities an outlier?

296. Does your organization of the data change its meaning?

297. Has management defined a definite timeframe for the turnaround or Security Consultants project window?

298. What is missing?

299. Activity: fair or not fair?

300. Which method produces the more accurate cost assignment?

301. Have you identified the Activity Leveling Priority code value on each activity?

302. How else could the items be grouped?

303. What conclusions/generalizations can you draw from this?

304. Do you feel very comfortable with your prediction?

305. Activity: what is In the Bag?

306. Can you re-assign any activities to another resource to resolve an over-allocation?

2.13 Milestone List: Security Consultants

307. Who will manage the Security Consultants project on a day-to-day basis?

308. Can you derive how soon can the whole Security Consultants project finish?

309. Vital contracts and partners?

310. Do you foresee any technical risks or developmental challenges?

311. It is to be a narrative text providing the crucial aspects of your Security Consultants project proposal answering what, who, how, when and where?

312. How will you get the word out to customers?

313. What has been done so far?

314. How late can each activity be finished and started?

315. Sustaining internal capabilities?

316. Level of the Innovation?

317. Legislative effects?

318. How will the milestone be verified?

319. Continuity, supply chain robustness?

320. New USPs?

321. How soon can the activity finish?

322. Timescales, deadlines and pressures?

323. How difficult will it be to do specific activities on this Security Consultants project?

324. Which path is the critical path?

325. Global influences?

2.14 Network Diagram: Security Consultants

326. What job or jobs precede it?

327. What job or jobs follow it?

328. How confident can you be in your milestone dates and the delivery date?

329. Can you calculate the confidence level?

330. What is the completion time?

331. Which type of network diagram allows you to depict four types of dependencies?

332. What job or jobs could run concurrently?

333. How difficult will it be to do specific activities on this Security Consultants project?

334. If a current contract exists, can you provide the vendor name, contract start, and contract expiration date?

335. Planning: who, how long, what to do?

336. Where do schedules come from?

337. Exercise: what is the probability that the Security Consultants project duration will exceed xx weeks?

338. What activities must follow this activity?

339. What is the probability of completing the Security Consultants project in less that xx days?

340. What activity must be completed immediately before this activity can start?

341. What to do and When?

342. Will crashing x weeks return more in benefits than it costs?

343. What controls the start and finish of a job?

2.15 Activity Resource Requirements: Security Consultants

344. Time for overtime?

345. When does monitoring begin?

346. What is the Work Plan Standard?

347. Organizational Applicability?

348. Anything else?

349. Other support in specific areas?

350. How do you manage time?

351. How many signatures do you require on a check and does this match what is in your policy and procedures?

352. Are there unresolved issues that need to be addressed?

353. Which logical relationship does the PDM use most often?

354. Do you use tools like decomposition and rolling-wave planning to produce the activity list and other outputs?

355. What are constraints that you might find during the Human Resource Planning process?

356. Why do you do that?

357. How do you handle petty cash?

2.16 Resource Breakdown Structure: Security Consultants

358. Who is allowed to see what data about which resources?

359. What are the requirements for resource data?

360. Who will be used as a Security Consultants project team member?

361. How difficult will it be to do specific activities on this Security Consultants project?

362. Which resources should be in the resource pool?

363. What can you do to improve productivity?

364. Changes based on input from stakeholders?

365. Why time management?

366. What defines a successful Security Consultants project?

367. What is each stakeholders desired outcome for the Security Consultants project?

368. Who will use the system?

369. Any changes from stakeholders?

370. What is the purpose of assigning and

documenting responsibility?

371. Who is allowed to perform which functions?

372. Who needs what information?

373. What is the number one predictor of a groups productivity?

374. What is Security Consultants project communication management?

2.17 Activity Duration Estimates: Security Consultants

375. What are the nine areas of expertise?

376. Is the work performed reviewed against contractual objectives?

377. Consider the examples of poor quality in information technology Security Consultants projects presented in the What Went Wrong?

378. Will it help promote wellness at your organization and reduce insurance costs?

379. (Cpi), and schedule performance index (spi) for the Security Consultants project?

380. What are the main types of goods and services being outsourced?

381. Which includes asking team members about the time estimates for activities and reaching agreement on the calendar date for each activity?

382. What type of contract was used and why?

383. If the optimiztic estimate for an activity is 12days, and the pessimistic estimate is 18days, what is the standard deviation of this activity?

384. Is a work breakdown structure created to organize and to confirm the scope of each Security

Consultants project?

385. What does it mean to take a systems view of a Security Consultants project?

386. Which suggestions do you find most useful?

387. What is the shortest possible time it will take to complete this Security Consultants project?

388. What is the duration of a milestone?

389. Which skills do you think are most important for an information technology Security Consultants project manager?

390. Do Security Consultants project team members work in the same physical location to enhance team performance?

391. Do your results resemble a normal distribution?

392. Research risk management software. Are many products available?

393. What Security Consultants project was the first to use modern Security Consultants project management?

394. Is training acquired to enhance the skills, knowledge and capabilities of the Security Consultants project team?

2.18 Duration Estimating Worksheet: Security Consultants

395. Why estimate costs?

396. What utility impacts are there?

397. Science = process: remember the scientific method?

398. Will the Security Consultants project collaborate with the local community and leverage resources?

399. What is an Average Security Consultants project?

400. What questions do you have?

401. What info is needed?

402. Is the Security Consultants project responsive to community need?

403. Why estimate time and cost?

404. Is a construction detail attached (to aid in explanation)?

405. Do any colleagues have experience with your organization and/or RFPs?

406. Does the Security Consultants project provide innovative ways for stakeholders to overcome obstacles or deliver better outcomes?

407. What is cost and Security Consultants project cost management?

408. What is the total time required to complete the Security Consultants project if no delays occur?

409. When does your organization expect to be able to complete it?

410. What is your role?

411. Value pocket identification & quantification what are value pockets?

2.19 Project Schedule: Security Consultants

412. Schedule/cost recovery?

413. How does a Security Consultants project get to be a year late ?

414. How effectively were issues able to be resolved without impacting the Security Consultants project Schedule or Budget?

415. How can slack be negative?

416. Is there a Schedule Management Plan that establishes the criteria and activities for developing, monitoring and controlling the Security Consultants project schedule?

417. Is Security Consultants project work proceeding in accordance with the original Security Consultants project schedule?

418. Why do you need schedules?

419. Have all Security Consultants project delays been adequately accounted for, communicated to all stakeholders and adjustments made in overall Security Consultants project schedule?

420. Was the Security Consultants project schedule reviewed by all stakeholders and formally accepted?

421. What does that mean?

422. Change management required?

423. What is the difference?

424. Are procedures defined by which the Security Consultants project schedule may be changed?

425. What is the most mis-scheduled part of process?

426. To what degree is do you feel the entire team was committed to the Security Consultants project schedule?

427. How do you know that youhave done this right?

428. Why is software Security Consultants project disaster so common?

429. Are key risk mitigation strategies added to the Security Consultants project schedule?

2.20 Cost Management Plan: Security Consultants

430. What would you do differently what did not work?

431. Is quality monitored from the perspective of the customers needs and expectations?

432. Is there anything unique in this Security Consultants projects scope statement that will affect resources?

433. Have stakeholder accountabilities & responsibilities been clearly defined?

434. Are change requests logged and managed?

435. Is there a formal set of procedures supporting Stakeholder Management?

436. Is your organization certified as a supplier, wholesaler, regular dealer, or manufacturer of corresponding products/supplies?

437. Are Security Consultants project contact logs kept up to date?

438. Pareto diagrams, statistical sampling, flow charting or trend analysis used quality monitoring?

439. Planning and scheduling responsibilities – How will the responsibilities for planning and scheduling

be allocated?

440. Are all key components of a Quality Assurance Plan present?

441. What is Security Consultants project cost management?

442. Resources – how will human resources be scheduled during each phase of the Security Consultants project?

443. Security Consultants project definition & scope?

444. What is an Acceptance Management Process?

445. Are enough systems & user personnel assigned to the Security Consultants project?

446. Milestones – what are the key dates in executing the contract plan?

447. Technical and functional?

2.21 Activity Cost Estimates: Security Consultants

448. What were things that you did very well and want to do the same again on the next Security Consultants project?

449. Eac -estimate at completion, what is the total job expected to cost?

450. Does the activity serve a common type of customer?

451. Why do you manage cost?

452. Review – what are some common errors in activities to avoid?

453. How do you change activities?

454. What is the Security Consultants projects sustainability strategy that will ensure Security Consultants project results will endure or be sustained?

455. In which phase of the acquisition process cycle does source qualifications reside?

456. How many activities should you have?

457. Were the tasks or work products prepared by the consultant useful?

458. Scope statement only direct or indirect costs as well?

459. Will you use any tools, such as Security Consultants project management software, to assist in capturing Earned Value metrics?

460. Measurable - are the targets measurable?

461. The impact and what actions were taken?

462. Can you change your activities?

463. Can you delete activities or make them inactive?

464. What skill level is required to do the job?

2.22 Cost Estimating Worksheet: Security Consultants

465. Ask: are others positioned to know, are others credible, and will others cooperate?

466. Can a trend be established from historical performance data on the selected measure and are the criteria for using trend analysis or forecasting methods met?

467. What is the estimated labor cost today based upon this information?

468. What costs are to be estimated?

469. Does the Security Consultants project provide innovative ways for stakeholders to overcome obstacles or deliver better outcomes?

470. What additional Security Consultants project(s) could be initiated as a result of this Security Consultants project?

471. How will the results be shared and to whom?

472. What happens to any remaining funds not used?

473. Is it feasible to establish a control group arrangement?

474. Is the Security Consultants project responsive to community need?

475. What is the purpose of estimating?

476. What will others want?

477. What can be included?

478. Will the Security Consultants project collaborate with the local community and leverage resources?

479. Who is best positioned to know and assist in identifying corresponding factors?

480. Identify the timeframe necessary to monitor progress and collect data to determine how the selected measure has changed?

2.23 Cost Baseline: Security Consultants

481. For what purpose ?

482. How concrete were original objectives?

483. On time?

484. Who will use corresponding metrics ?

485. Are procedures defined by which the cost baseline may be changed?

486. Have the actual milestone completion dates been compared to the approved schedule?

487. Have you identified skills that are missing from your team?

488. How long are you willing to wait before you find out were late?

489. Should a more thorough impact analysis be conducted?

490. What threats might prevent you from getting there?

491. Have the lessons learned been filed with the Security Consultants project Management Office?

492. Pcs for your new business. what would the life

cycle costs be?

493. Impact to environment?

494. How difficult will it be to do specific tasks on the Security Consultants project?

495. What do you want to measure ?

496. What deliverables come first?

497. Have the resources used by the Security Consultants project been reassigned to other units or Security Consultants projects?

498. Is request in line with priorities?

499. Have all approved changes to the cost baseline been identified and impact on the Security Consultants project documented?

2.24 Quality Management Plan: Security Consultants

500. How do you ensure that your sampling methods and procedures meet your data quality objectives?

501. How does your organization design processes to ensure others meet customer and others requirements?

502. Is there a Quality Management Plan?

503. Would impacts defined serve as impediments?

504. Has a Security Consultants project Communications Plan been developed?

505. How are calibration records kept?

506. Who needs a qmp?

507. How does your organization manage work to promote cooperation, individual initiative, innovation, flexibility, communications, and knowledge/skill sharing across work units?

508. How does your organization manage training and evaluate its effectiveness?

509. How does your organization use comparative data and information to improve organizational performance?

510. No superfluous information or marketing narrative?

511. Account for the procedures used to verify the data quality of the data being reviewed?

512. Have adequate resources been provided by management to ensure Security Consultants project success?

513. Is the steering committee active in Security Consultants project oversight?

514. How do you manage quality?

515. Modifications to the requirements?

516. Who is approving the QAPP?

517. How do you field-modify testing procedures?

2.25 Quality Metrics: Security Consultants

518. Did the team meet the Security Consultants project success criteria documented in the Quality Metrics Matrix?

519. There are many reasons to shore up quality-related metrics, and what metrics are important?

520. What is the timeline to meet your goal?

521. Has risk analysis been adequately reviewed?

522. How do you calculate corresponding metrics?

523. Is quality culture a competitive advantage?

524. Are interface issues coordinated?

525. What are your organizations next steps?

526. Was the overall quality better or worse than previous products?

527. Was review conducted per standard protocols?

528. Which are the right metrics to use?

529. What does this tell us?

530. What is the benchmark?

531. What level of statistical confidence do you use?

532. Are there already quality metrics available that detect nonlinear embeddings and trends similar to the users perception?

533. What can manufacturing professionals do to ensure quality is seen as an integral part of the entire product lifecycle?

534. What method of measurement do you use?

535. Do you stratify metrics by product or site?

536. Is there a set of procedures to capture, analyze and act on quality metrics?

537. Has trace of defects been initiated?

2.26 Process Improvement Plan: Security Consultants

538. Does your process ensure quality?

539. Management commitment at all levels?

540. What personnel are the champions for the initiative?

541. Purpose of goal: the motive is determined by asking, why do you want to achieve this goal?

542. What personnel are the change agents for your initiative?

543. Why quality management?

544. Has the time line required to move measurement results from the points of collection to databases or users been established?

545. Are you making progress on the improvement framework?

546. To elicit goal statements, do you ask a question such as, What do you want to achieve?

547. Why do you want to achieve the goal?

548. Are there forms and procedures to collect and record the data?

549. Where do you want to be?

550. Has a process guide to collect the data been developed?

551. What lessons have you learned so far?

552. What personnel are the sponsors for that initiative?

553. Where are you now?

554. Are you making progress on your improvement plan?

555. Does explicit definition of the measures exist?

556. What is the return on investment?

2.27 Responsibility Assignment Matrix: Security Consultants

557. Performance to date and material commitment?

558. Are your organizations and items of cost assigned to each pool identified?

559. What are the deliverables?

560. How do you assist them to be as productive as possible?

561. What do you need to implement earned value management?

562. Are all authorized tasks assigned to identified organizational elements?

563. Are the actual costs used for variance analysis reconcilable with data from the accounting system?

564. Is work properly classified as measured effort, LOE, or apportioned effort and appropriately separated?

565. What happens when others get pulled for higher priority Security Consultants projects?

566. Does the Security Consultants project need to be analyzed further to uncover additional responsibilities?

567. Are people encouraged to bring up issues?

568. Are others working on the right things?

569. When performing is split among two or more roles, is the work clearly defined so that the efforts are coordinated and the communication is clear?

570. Are work packages assigned to performing organizations?

571. Who is responsible for work and budgets for each wbs?

2.28 Roles and Responsibilities: Security Consultants

572. Are governance roles and responsibilities documented?

573. Are Security Consultants project team roles and responsibilities identified and documented?

574. To decide whether to use a quality measurement, ask how will you know when it is achieved?

575. Where are you most strong as a supervisor?

576. Does the team have access to and ability to use data analysis tools?

577. What expectations were met?

578. What should you highlight for improvement?

579. What is working well?

580. How well did the Security Consultants project Team understand the expectations of specific roles and responsibilities?

581. Do you take the time to clearly define roles and responsibilities on Security Consultants project tasks?

582. What should you do now to prepare for your career 5+ years from now?

583. Are the quality assurance functions and related roles and responsibilities clearly defined?

584. Is there a training program in place for stakeholders covering expectations, roles and responsibilities and any addition knowledge others need to be good stakeholders?

585. How is your work-life balance?

586. Are your budgets supportive of a culture of quality data?

587. What specific behaviors did you observe?

588. Is feedback clearly communicated and non-judgmental?

589. What should you do now to ensure that you are meeting all expectations of your current position?

2.29 Human Resource Management Plan: Security Consultants

590. Are vendor contract reports, reviews and visits conducted periodically?

591. Are the people assigned to the Security Consultants project sufficiently qualified?

592. Is pert / critical path or equivalent methodology being used?

593. Are the key elements of a Security Consultants project Charter present?

594. Does the Security Consultants project have a Statement of Work?

595. Is your organization heading towards expansion, outsourcing of certain talents or making cut-backs to save money?

596. Are tasks tracked by hours?

597. Are post milestone Security Consultants project reviews (PMPR) conducted with your organization at least once a year?

598. Are changes in deliverable commitments agreed to by all affected groups & individuals?

599. Are parking lot items captured?

600. Are quality inspections and review activities listed in the Security Consultants project schedule(s)?

601. Are people being developed to meet the challenges of the future?

602. Is Security Consultants project work proceeding in accordance with the original Security Consultants project schedule?

603. Are Security Consultants project contact logs kept up to date?

604. Have lessons learned been conducted after each Security Consultants project release?

605. Are people motivated to meet the current and future challenges?

606. Alignment to strategic goals & objectives?

607. Have all unresolved risks been documented?

608. Are Security Consultants project team members involved in detailed estimating and scheduling?

609. Is the steering committee active in Security Consultants project oversight?

2.30 Communications Management Plan: Security Consultants

610. Is there an important stakeholder who is actively opposed and will not receive messages?

611. What is the stakeholders level of authority?

612. What to know?

613. Are others part of the communications management plan?

614. Timing: when do the effects of the communication take place?

615. How often do you engage with stakeholders?

616. Who to learn from?

617. Do you prepare stakeholder engagement plans?

618. What to learn?

619. How is this initiative related to other portfolios, programs, or Security Consultants projects?

620. Who were proponents/opponents?

621. Do you then often overlook a key stakeholder or stakeholder group?

622. Are the stakeholders getting the information

others need, are others consulted, are concerns addressed?

623. How did the term stakeholder originate?

624. Will messages be directly related to the release strategy or phases of the Security Consultants project?

625. Who needs to know and how much?

626. Who have you worked with in past, similar initiatives?

627. What does the stakeholder need from the team?

628. Who is the stakeholder?

2.31 Risk Management Plan: Security Consultants

629. Is Security Consultants project scope stable?

630. Have you worked with the customer in the past?

631. Are the reports useful and easy to read?

632. Why do you want risk management?

633. Risk probability and impact: how will the probabilities and impacts of risk items be assessed?

634. Degree of confidence in estimated size estimate?

635. Is the process being followed?

636. Who/what can assist?

637. Which risks should get the attention?

638. Has something like this been done before?

639. Are team members trained in the use of the tools?

640. What is the likelihood?

641. Are certain activities taking a long time to complete?

642. Is the necessary data being captured and is it

complete and accurate?

643. How are risk analvsis and prioritization performed?

644. What risks are tracked?

645. Does the software engineering team have the right mix of skills?

646. Methodology: how will risk management be performed on this Security Consultants project?

647. Risks should be identified during which phase of Security Consultants project management life cycle?

2.32 Risk Register: Security Consultants

648. Why would you develop a risk register?

649. Budget and schedule: what are the estimated costs and schedules for performing risk-related activities?

650. Preventative actions - planned actions to reduce the likelihood a risk will occur and/or reduce the seriousness should it occur. What should you do now?

651. What will be done?

652. Manageability – have mitigations to the risk been identified?

653. When would you develop a risk register?

654. What is a Community Risk Register?

655. How are risks graded?

656. Who is going to do it?

657. Methodology: how will risk management be performed on this Security Consultants project?

658. Can the likelihood and impact of failing to achieve corresponding recommendations and action plans be assessed?

659. What should you do now?

660. Do you require further engagement?

661. How are risks identified?

662. Assume the event happens, what is the Most Likely impact?

663. People risk -are people with appropriate skills available to help complete the Security Consultants project?

664. Amongst the action plans and recommendations that you have to introduce are there some that could stop or delay the overall program?

665. When will it happen?

666. Are there other alternative controls that could be implemented?

667. Cost/benefit – how much will the proposed mitigations cost and how does this cost compare with the potential cost of the risk event/situation should it occur?

2.33 Probability and Impact Assessment: Security Consultants

668. What are the uncertainties associated with the technology selected for the Security Consultants project?

669. Are the facilities, expertise, resources, and management know-how available to handle the situation?

670. Will new information become available during the Security Consultants project?

671. What are the probabilities of chosen technologies being suitable for local conditions?

672. How much is the probability of a risk occurring?

673. How is the Security Consultants project going to be managed?

674. Management -what contingency plans do you have if the risk becomes a reality?

675. Is the customer willing to establish rapid communication links with the developer?

676. What should be the gestation period for the Security Consultants project with specific technology?

677. How solid is the Security Consultants projection of competitive reaction?

678. Are there any Security Consultants projects similar to this one in existence?

679. How completely has the customer been identified?

680. How well is the risk understood?

681. Have top software and customer managers formally committed to support the Security Consultants project?

682. Can it be enlarged by drawing people from other areas of your organization?

683. How risk averse are you?

684. What action do you usually take against risks?

685. Can the risk be avoided by choosing a different alternative?

686. What is the Security Consultants project managers level of commitment and professionalism?

687. What should be done with non-critical risks?

2.34 Probability and Impact Matrix: Security Consultants

688. Which should be probably done NEXT?

689. Which phase of the Security Consultants project do you take part in?

690. Prioritized components/features?

691. What is the political situation at present?

692. Which role do you have in the Security Consultants project?

693. What needs to be DONE?

694. Are tool mentors available?

695. Is the Security Consultants project cutting across the entire organization?

696. What are the channels available for distribution to the customer?

697. What will be cost of redeployment of the personnel?

698. Does the customer have a solid idea of what is required?

699. Which is an input to the risk management process?

700. What are the current or emerging trends of culture?

701. What will be the impact or consequence if the risk occurs?

702. Could others have been better mitigated?

703. How is the Security Consultants project going to be managed?

704. Do you know the order of planning yet?

2.35 Risk Data Sheet: Security Consultants

705. What if client refuses?

706. What are the main opportunities available to you that you should grab while you can?

707. What are the main threats to your existence?

708. Will revised controls lead to tolerable risk levels?

709. What are your core values?

710. What actions can be taken to eliminate or remove risk?

711. What are you weak at and therefore need to do better?

712. How do you handle product safely?

713. How reliable is the data source?

714. Type of risk identified?

715. Potential for recurrence?

716. What is the chance that it will happen?

717. If it happens, what are the consequences?

718. What will be the consequences if the risk

happens?

719. Do effective diagnostic tests exist?

720. Has the most cost-effective solution been chosen?

721. What can happen?

722. Risk of what?

723. Whom do you serve (customers)?

724. What is the environment within which you operate (social trends, economic, community values, broad based participation, national directions etc.)?

2.36 Procurement Management Plan: Security Consultants

725. What is the last item a Security Consultants project manager must do to finalize Security Consultants project close-out?

726. Is it standard practice to formally commit stakeholders to the Security Consultants project via agreements?

727. Has a provision been made to reassess Security Consultants project risks at various Security Consultants project stages?

728. Has a quality assurance plan been developed for the Security Consultants project?

729. Do Security Consultants project managers participating in the Security Consultants project know the Security Consultants projects true status first hand?

730. Are the key elements of a Security Consultants project Charter present?

731. Were escalated issues resolved promptly?

732. Why is procurement planning important?

733. What are things that you need to improve?

734. Sensitivity analysis?

735. Is the schedule updated on a periodic basis?

736. Are the budget estimates reasonable?

737. Are the quality tools and methods identified in the Quality Plan appropriate to the Security Consultants project?

738. Have the key elements of a coherent Security Consultants project management strategy been established?

739. Is the communication plan being followed?

740. Are metrics used to evaluate and manage Vendors?

2.37 Source Selection Criteria: Security Consultants

741. How and when do you enter into Security Consultants project Procurement Management?

742. What are the steps in performing a cost/tech tradeoff?

743. How is past performance evaluated?

744. How do you encourage efficiency and consistency?

745. Do you prepare an independent cost estimate?

746. Has all proposal data been loaded?

747. What information may not be provided?

748. How will you evaluate offerors proposals?

749. In order of importance, which evaluation criteria are the most critical to the determination of your overall rating?

750. What should a Draft Request for Proposal (DRFP) include?

751. How should comments received in response to a RFP be handled?

752. Will the technical evaluation factor unnecessarily

force the acquisition into a higher-priced market segment?

753. What should be the contracting officers strategy?

754. What is price analysis and when should it be performed?

755. What are open book debriefings?

756. Do you want to wait until all offerors have been evaluated?

757. Do proposed hours support content and schedule?

758. Are resultant proposal revisions allowed?

759. What common questions or problems are associated with debriefings?

760. How organization are proposed quotes/prices?

2.38 Stakeholder Management Plan: Security Consultants

761. Has the Security Consultants project manager been identified?

762. Who will be responsible for managing and maintaining the Issues Register?

763. How will the equipment be verified?

764. Does the Security Consultants project have a Quality Culture?

765. What is positive about the current process?

766. Do Security Consultants project teams & team members report on status / activities / progress?

767. Does the business case include how the Security Consultants project aligns with your organizations strategic goals & objectives?

768. Are action items captured and managed?

769. What is the process for purchases that arent acceptable (eg damaged goods)?

770. What would you gain if you spent time working to improve this process?

771. Are schedule deliverables actually delivered?

772. Are software metrics formally captured, analyzed and used as a basis for other Security Consultants project estimates?

773. Will all relevant stakeholders be included within the review process?

774. How are you doing/what can be done better?

775. Is the current scope of the Security Consultants project substantially different than that originally defined?

776. Who is responsible for the post implementation review process?

777. What other teams / processes would be impacted by changes to the current process, and how?

2.39 Change Management Plan: Security Consultants

778. Identify the risk and assess the significance and likelihood of it occurring and plan the contingency What risks may occur upfront?

779. Who will fund the training?

780. Do you need new systems?

781. Do the proposed users have access to the appropriate documentation?

782. What would be an estimate of the total cost for the activities required to carry out the change initiative?

783. How frequently should you repeat the message?

784. What policies and procedures need to be changed?

785. What prerequisite knowledge or training is required?

786. Will all field readiness criteria have been practically met prior to training roll-out?

787. Who should be involved in developing a change management strategy?

788. Has a training need analysis been carried out?

789. Is there support for this application(s) and are the details available for distribution?

790. Where will the funds come from?

791. Has an information & communications plan been developed?

792. Are there any restrictions on who can receive the communications?

793. Are work location changes required?

794. Who might be able to help you the most?

795. What risks may occur upfront, during implementation and after implementation?

796. What new behaviours are required?

797. What are the dependencies?

3.0 Executing Process Group: Security Consultants

798. Does software appear easy to learn?

799. How could stakeholders negatively impact your Security Consultants project?

800. How do you enter durations, link tasks, and view critical path information?

801. Is the Security Consultants project making progress in helping to achieve the set results?

802. Is the Security Consultants project performing better or worse than planned?

803. Could a new application negatively affect the current IT infrastructure?

804. Is the schedule for the set products being met?

805. How does Security Consultants project management relate to other disciplines?

806. What will you do to minimize the impact should a risk event occur?

807. Does the Security Consultants project team have the right skills?

808. How well defined and documented were the Security Consultants project management processes

you chose to use?

809. What communication items need improvement?

810. Does the case present a realistic scenario?

811. Do the products created live up to the necessary quality?

812. When will the Security Consultants project be done?

813. It under budget or over budget?

814. Specific - is the objective clear in terms of what, how, when, and where the situation will be changed?

815. When is the appropriate time to bring the scorecard to Board meetings?

3.1 Team Member Status Report: Security Consultants

816. How much risk is involved?

817. Will the staff do training or is that done by a third party?

818. Is there evidence that staff is taking a more professional approach toward management of your organizations Security Consultants projects?

819. How it is to be done?

820. How does this product, good, or service meet the needs of the Security Consultants project and your organization as a whole?

821. Does every department have to have a Security Consultants project Manager on staff?

822. Do you have an Enterprise Security Consultants project Management Office (EPMO)?

823. Does the product, good, or service already exist within your organization?

824. Are your organizations Security Consultants projects more successful over time?

825. Are the attitudes of staff regarding Security Consultants project work improving?

826. Does your organization have the means (staff, money, contract, etc.) to produce or to acquire the product, good, or service?

827. Are the products of your organizations Security Consultants projects meeting customers objectives?

828. What is to be done?

829. What specific interest groups do you have in place?

830. When a teams productivity and success depend on collaboration and the efficient flow of information, what generally fails them?

831. Why is it to be done?

832. How will resource planning be done?

833. How can you make it practical?

834. The problem with Reward & Recognition Programs is that the truly deserving people all too often get left out. How can you make it practical?

3.2 Change Request: Security Consultants

835. What has an inspector to inspect and to check?

836. What mechanism is used to appraise others of changes that are made?

837. Screen shots or attachments included in a Change Request?

838. Who is included in the change control team?

839. Have scm procedures for noting the change, recording it, and reporting it been followed?

840. Who is responsible to authorize changes?

841. How to get changes (code) out in a timely manner?

842. Why do you want to have a change control system?

843. Will all change requests be unconditionally tracked through this process?

844. How does a team identify the discrete elements of a configuration?

845. How well do experienced software developers predict software change?

846. Can you answer what happened, who did it, when did it happen, and what else will be affected?

847. For which areas does this operating procedure apply?

848. What must be taken into consideration when introducing change control programs?

849. Who is responsible for the implementation and monitoring of all measures?

850. Who is communicating the change?

851. Change request coordination ?

852. What are the requirements for urgent changes?

853. What is the relationship between requirements attributes and reliability?

854. How is the change documented (format, content, storage)?

3.3 Change Log: Security Consultants

855. Do the described changes impact on the integrity or security of the system?

856. Will the Security Consultants project fail if the change request is not executed?

857. Does the suggested change request seem to represent a necessary enhancement to the product?

858. Does the suggested change request represent a desired enhancement to the products functionality?

859. When was the request approved?

860. Is the change request open, closed or pending?

861. Is the requested change request a result of changes in other Security Consultants project(s)?

862. Who initiated the change request?

863. Is the change backward compatible without limitations?

864. How does this change affect the timeline of the schedule?

865. When was the request submitted?

866. Is the change request within Security Consultants project scope?

867. Is this a mandatory replacement?

868. How does this relate to the standards developed for specific business processes?

869. Is the submitted change a new change or a modification of a previously approved change?

870. How does this change affect scope?

871. Where do changes come from?

3.4 Decision Log: Security Consultants

872. How does the use a Decision Support System influence the strategies/tactics or costs?

873. What eDiscovery problem or issue did your organization set out to fix or make better?

874. What is the line where eDiscovery ends and document review begins?

875. How consolidated and comprehensive a story can you tell by capturing currently available incident data in a central location and through a log of key decisions during an incident?

876. Is everything working as expected?

877. How do you know when you are achieving it?

878. Who will be given a copy of this document and where will it be kept?

879. It becomes critical to track and periodically revisit both operational effectiveness; Are you noticing all that you need to, and are you interpreting what you see effectively?

880. With whom was the decision shared or considered?

881. Linked to original objective?

882. Is your opponent open to a non-traditional

workflow, or will it likely challenge anything you do?

883. Do strategies and tactics aimed at less than full control reduce the costs of management or simply shift the cost burden?

884. What alternatives/risks were considered?

885. How does an increasing emphasis on cost containment influence the strategies and tactics used?

886. How effective is maintaining the log at facilitating organizational learning?

887. Adversarial environment. is your opponent open to a non-traditional workflow, or will it likely challenge anything you do?

888. How do you define success?

889. At what point in time does loss become unacceptable?

890. Does anything need to be adjusted?

891. Behaviors; what are guidelines that the team has identified that will assist them with getting the most out of team meetings?

3.5 Quality Audit: Security Consultants

892. How does your organization know that its management of its ethical responsibilities is appropriately effective and constructive?

893. Is progress against the intentions measurable?

894. How does your organization know that its Mission, Vision and Values Statements are appropriate and effectively guiding your organization?

895. How does your organization ensure that equipment is appropriately maintained and producing valid results?

896. Is your organizations resource allocation system properly aligned with its collection of intentions?

897. Is there a written procedure for receiving materials?

898. How does your organization know whether they are adhering to mission and achieving objectives?

899. Are training programs documented?

900. What are your supplier audits?

901. How does your organization know that its systems for communicating with and among staff are appropriately effective and constructive?

902. How does your organization know that its system for governing staff behaviour is appropriately effective and constructive?

903. Does the supplier use a formal quality system?

904. Is the process of self review, learning and improvement endemic throughout your organization?

905. What does an analysis of your organizations staff profile suggest in terms of its planning, and how is this being addressed?

906. Are multiple statements on the same issue consistent with each other?

907. How does your organization know that the support for its staff is appropriately effective and constructive?

908. How does your organization know that its methods are appropriately effective and constructive?

909. What is the collective experience of the team to be assigned to an audit?

910. Are measuring and test equipment that have been placed out of service suitably identified and excluded from use in any device reconditioning operation?

3.6 Team Directory: Security Consultants

911. What needs to be communicated?

912. Who are your stakeholders (customers, sponsors, end users, team members)?

913. Contract requirements complied with?

914. Who will write the meeting minutes and distribute?

915. How and in what format should information be presented?

916. Who will be the stakeholders on your next Security Consultants project?

917. Process decisions: are all start-up, turn over and close out requirements of the contract satisfied?

918. What are you going to deliver or accomplish?

919. Have you decided when to celebrate the Security Consultants projects completion date?

920. Who are the Team Members?

921. Process decisions: do job conditions warrant additional actions to collect job information and document on-site activity?

922. How will you accomplish and manage the objectives?

923. Decisions: is the most suitable form of contract being used?

924. Process decisions: are there any statutory or regulatory issues relevant to the timely execution of work?

925. Who should receive information (all stakeholders)?

926. Days from the time the issue is identified?

927. When will you produce deliverables?

928. Process decisions: do invoice amounts match accepted work in place?

929. Process decisions: are contractors adequately prosecuting the work?

3.7 Team Operating Agreement: Security Consultants

930. Do you leverage technology engagement tools group chat, polls, screen sharing, etc.?

931. The method to be used in the decision making process; Will it be consensus, majority rule, or the supervisor having the final say?

932. Communication protocols: how will the team communicate?

933. Are there influences outside the team that may affect performance, and if so, have you identified and addressed them?

934. Do you ask participants to close laptops and place mobile devices on silent on the table while the meeting is in progress?

935. What is culture?

936. What went well?

937. Does your team need access to all documents and information at all times?

938. Do you ensure that all participants know how to use the required technology?

939. What is a Virtual Team?

940. How will you resolve conflict efficiently and respectfully?

941. Resource allocation: how will individual team members account for time and expenses, and how will this be allocated in the team budget?

942. Do you record meetings for the already stated unable to attend?

943. Must your members collaborate successfully to complete Security Consultants projects?

944. Are leadership responsibilities shared among team members (versus a single leader)?

945. Have you set the goals and objectives of the team?

946. Are team roles clearly defined and accepted?

947. Do you post any action items, due dates, and responsibilities on the team website?

948. To whom do you deliver your services?

949. What individual strengths does each team member bring to the group?

3.8 Team Performance Assessment: Security Consultants

950. To what degree is there a sense that only the team can succeed?

951. What is method variance?

952. Can familiarity breed backup?

953. To what degree are the members clear on what they are individually responsible for and what they are jointly responsible for?

954. What are teams?

955. To what degree does the teams work approach provide opportunity for members to engage in fact-based problem solving?

956. Does more radicalness mean more perceived benefits?

957. To what degree are the teams goals and objectives clear, simple, and measurable?

958. To what degree do members understand and articulate the same purpose without relying on ambiguous abstractions?

959. Where to from here?

960. To what degree can team members meet

frequently enough to accomplish the teams ends?

961. What structural changes have you made or are you preparing to make?

962. To what degree does the teams approach to its work allow for modification and improvement over time?

963. To what degree does the team possess adequate membership to achieve its ends?

964. To what degree will the team adopt a concrete, clearly understood, and agreed-upon approach that will result in achievement of the teams goals?

965. Which situations call for a more extreme type of adaptiveness in which team members actually re-define roles?

966. To what degree are fresh input and perspectives systematically caught and added (for example, through information and analysis, new members, and senior sponsors)?

967. To what degree are the skill areas critical to team performance present?

968. To what degree are the goals ambitious?

969. To what degree can all members engage in open and interactive considerations?

3.9 Team Member Performance Assessment: Security Consultants

970. Why do performance reviews?

971. What are the staffs preferences for training on technology-based platforms?

972. How do you create a self-sustaining capacity for a collaborative culture?

973. Are assessment validation activities performed?

974. Are any governance changes sufficient to impact achievement?

975. For what period of time is a member rated?

976. What kinds of performance factors / elements do you use?

977. How do you determine which data are the most important to use, analyze, or review?

978. How are assessments designed, delivered, and otherwise used to maximize training?

979. Does the rater (supervisor) have to wait for the interim or final performance assessment review to tell an employee that the employees performance is unsatisfactory?

980. What, if any, steps are available for employees

who feel they have been unfairly or inaccurately rated?

981. How do you start collaborating?

982. Does platform-specific assessment information contribute to training placement or tailoring of instruction (e.g. aptitude-treatment interaction)?

983. To what degree do team members understand one anothers roles and skills?

984. To what extent are systems and applications (e.g., game engine, mobile device platform) utilized?

985. How is performance assessment used in making future award decisions including options and extend/ compete decisions?

986. How are performance measures and associated incentives developed?

3.10 Issue Log: Security Consultants

987. What help do you and your team need from the stakeholders?

988. Which stakeholders can influence others?

989. Is access to the Issue Log controlled?

990. Are there common objectives between the team and the stakeholder?

991. How were past initiatives successful?

992. What steps can you take for positive relationships?

993. What is a Stakeholder?

994. Do you feel more overwhelmed by stakeholders?

995. Are the Security Consultants project issues uniquely identified, including to which product they refer?

996. What is the impact on the Business Case?

997. Are you constantly rushing from meeting to meeting?

998. Can you think of other people who might have concerns or interests?

999. How do you reply to this question; you am new

here and managing this major program. How do you suggest you build your network?

1000. Which stakeholders are thought leaders, influences, or early adopters?

1001. Why do you manage human resources?

1002. In classifying stakeholders, which approach to do so are you using?

4.0 Monitoring and Controlling Process Group: Security Consultants

1003. Use: how will they use the information?

1004. In what way has the program come up with innovative measures for problem-solving?

1005. How were collaborations developed, and how are they sustained?

1006. Did you implement the program as designed?

1007. Where is the Risk in the Security Consultants project?

1008. Mitigate. what will you do to minimize the impact should a risk event occur?

1009. When will the Security Consultants project be done?

1010. How to ensure validity, quality and consistency?

1011. Is there adequate validation on required fields?

1012. What areas does the group agree are the biggest success on the Security Consultants project?

1013. Change, where should you look for problems?

1014. What are the goals of the program?

1015. Did it work?

1016. What were things that you did well, and could improve, and how?

1017. How well did the chosen processes fit the needs of the Security Consultants project?

1018. Just how important is your work to the overall success of the Security Consultants project?

1019. How well did you do?

1020. Is the program making progress in helping to achieve the set results?

1021. Does the solution fit in with organizations technical architectural requirements?

4.1 Project Performance Report: Security Consultants

1022. To what degree are the tasks requirements reflected in the flow and storage of information?

1023. To what degree can the cognitive capacity of individuals accommodate the flow of information?

1024. To what degree does the information network provide individuals with the information they require?

1025. To what degree do members articulate the goals beyond the team membership?

1026. What is the PRS?

1027. To what degree do the structures of the formal organization motivate taskrelevant behavior and facilitate task completion?

1028. To what degree will the team ensure that all members equitably share the work essential to the success of the team?

1029. To what degree will each member have the opportunity to advance his or her professional skills in all three of the above categories while contributing to the accomplishment of the teams purpose and goals?

1030. To what degree will the approach capitalize on and enhance the skills of all team members in a manner that takes into consideration other demands on members of the team?

1031. To what degree are sub-teams possible or necessary?

1032. To what degree are the demands of the task compatible with and converge with the relationships of the informal organization?

1033. What is the degree to which rules govern information exchange between groups?

1034. To what degree is there centralized control of information sharing?

1035. To what degree does the informal organization make use of individual resources and meet individual needs?

1036. How will procurement be coordinated with other Security Consultants project aspects, such as scheduling and performance reporting?

1037. What degree are the relative importance and priority of the goals clear to all team members?

4.2 Variance Analysis: Security Consultants

1038. Are the requirements for all items of overhead established by rational, traceable processes?

1039. Did a new competitor enter the market?

1040. Is the market likely to continue to grow at this rate next year?

1041. Can process improvements lead to unfavorable variances?

1042. Are all elements of indirect expense identified to overhead cost budgets of Security Consultants projections?

1043. Are the bases and rates for allocating costs from each indirect pool consistently applied?

1044. Are indirect costs accumulated for comparison with the corresponding budgets?

1045. What types of services and expense are shared between business segments?

1046. Are procedures for variance analysis documented and consistently applied at the control account level and selected WBS and organizational levels at least monthly as a routine task?

1047. Are there externalities from having some

customers, even if they are unprofitable in the short run?

1048. What costs are avoidable if one or more customers are dropped?

1049. Why do variances exist?

1050. Contemplated overhead expenditure for each period based on the best information currently is available?

1051. How do you identify and isolate causes of favorable and unfavorable cost and schedule variances?

1052. What is the performance to date and material commitment?

1053. Does the contractors system include procedures for measuring the performance of critical subcontractors?

1054. Who are responsible for overhead performance control of related costs?

1055. Are there changes in the overhead pool and/or organization structures?

4.3 Earned Value Status: Security Consultants

1056. When is it going to finish?

1057. How much is it going to cost by the finish?

1058. If earned value management (EVM) is so good in determining the true status of a Security Consultants project and Security Consultants project its completion, why is it that hardly any one uses it in information systems related Security Consultants projects?

1059. Verification is a process of ensuring that the developed system satisfies the stakeholders agreements and specifications; Are you building the product right? What do you verify?

1060. How does this compare with other Security Consultants projects?

1061. Are you hitting your Security Consultants projects targets?

1062. Validation is a process of ensuring that the developed system will actually achieve the stakeholders desired outcomes; Are you building the right product? What do you validate?

1063. What is the unit of forecast value?

1064. Earned value can be used in almost any Security

Consultants project situation and in almost any Security Consultants project environment. it may be used on large Security Consultants projects, medium sized Security Consultants projects, tiny Security Consultants projects (in cut-down form), complex and simple Security Consultants projects and in any market sector. some people, of course, know all about earned value, they have used it for years - but perhaps not as effectively as they could have?

1065. Where are your problem areas?

1066. Where is evidence-based earned value in your organization reported?

4.4 Risk Audit: Security Consultants

1067. Are corresponding safety and risk management policies posted for all to see?

1068. Can analytical tests provide evidence that is as strong as evidence from traditional substantive tests?

1069. To what extent are auditors influenced by the business risk assessment in the audit process, and how can auditors create more effective mental models to more fully examine contradictory evidence?

1070. What is happening in other jurisdictions? Could that happen here?

1071. What are the benefits of a Enterprise wide approach to Risk Management?

1072. Is the technology to be built new to your organization?

1073. Do you record and file all audits?

1074. What does internal control mean in the context of the audit process?

1075. Does your organization meet the terms of any contracts with which it is involved?

1076. Do you have proper induction processes for all new paid staff and volunteers who have a specific role and responsibility?

1077. Are you meeting your legal, regulatory and compliance requirements - if not, why not?

1078. Do you have a mechanism for managing change?

1079. Are all programs planned and conducted according to recognized safety standards?

1080. Which assets are important?

1081. Are risk assessments documented?

1082. If applicable; which route/packaging option do you choose for transport of hazmat material?

1083. Are you willing to seek legal advice when required?

1084. Does the implementation method matter?

1085. What is the Board doing to assure measurement and improve outcomes and quality and reduce avoidable adverse events?

4.5 Contractor Status Report: Security Consultants

1086. What was the overall budget or estimated cost?

1087. What was the final actual cost?

1088. Who can list a Security Consultants project as organization experience, your organization or a previous employee of your organization?

1089. Describe how often regular updates are made to the proposed solution. Are corresponding regular updates included in the standard maintenance plan?

1090. What was the budget or estimated cost for your organizations services?

1091. What process manages the contracts?

1092. Are there contractual transfer concerns?

1093. How is risk transferred?

1094. How long have you been using the services?

1095. What was the actual budget or estimated cost for your organizations services?

1096. What is the average response time for answering a support call?

1097. What are the minimum and optimal bandwidth

requirements for the proposed solution?

1098. If applicable; describe your standard schedule for new software version releases. Are new software version releases included in the standard maintenance plan?

4.6 Formal Acceptance: Security Consultants

1099. Is formal acceptance of the Security Consultants project product documented and distributed?

1100. Do you buy pre-configured systems or build your own configuration?

1101. What are the requirements against which to test, Who will execute?

1102. What was done right?

1103. Do you perform formal acceptance or burn-in tests?

1104. How well did the team follow the methodology?

1105. Was business value realized?

1106. What lessons were learned about your Security Consultants project management methodology?

1107. Did the Security Consultants project achieve its MOV?

1108. Does it do what client said it would?

1109. Was the Security Consultants project managed well?

1110. Who supplies data?

1111. What function(s) does it fill or meet?

1112. Who would use it?

1113. What features, practices, and processes proved to be strengths or weaknesses?

1114. General estimate of the costs and times to complete the Security Consultants project?

1115. Was the Security Consultants project goal achieved?

1116. What is the Acceptance Management Process?

1117. Was the sponsor/customer satisfied?

1118. What can you do better next time?

5.0 Closing Process Group: Security Consultants

1119. How well defined and documented were the Security Consultants project management processes you chose to use?

1120. What areas were overlooked on this Security Consultants project?

1121. What will you do?

1122. Was the schedule met?

1123. Is the Security Consultants project funded?

1124. Were sponsors and decision makers available when needed outside regularly scheduled meetings?

1125. Is the Security Consultants project funded?

1126. Just how important is your work to the overall success of the Security Consultants project?

1127. Is this a follow-on to a previous Security Consultants project?

1128. Was the user/client satisfied with the end product?

1129. Did you do things well?

1130. What were the desired outcomes?

1131. Did the Security Consultants project team have the right skills?

1132. When will the Security Consultants project be done?

1133. What is the amount of funding and what Security Consultants project phases are funded?

1134. What were the actual outcomes?

1135. What is the overall risk of the Security Consultants project to your organization?

1136. What level of risk does the proposed budget represent to the Security Consultants project?

1137. Were cost budgets met?

5.1 Procurement Audit: Security Consultants

1138. How do you ensure whether the goods were supplied or works executed in time and properly recorded in measurement books and stock/works registers after inspection?

1139. Are individuals with check-signing responsibility prohibited from signing blank checks?

1140. Are all checks stored in a secure area?

1141. Are services/tasks combined in such a way that the market is used where relevant?

1142. Did additional works amount to no more than 50% of the initial contract?

1143. How do you avoid delays at any stage/ stages of the procurement process?

1144. What are your ethical guidelines for public procurement?

1145. Is the purchasing department facility laid out to facilitate interviews with salespersons?

1146. Was the admissibility of variants displayed in the contract notice?

1147. Are there internal control systems in place to secure that laws and regulations are observed?

1148. Are all claims certified by the officer giving rise to the claim (usually the purchasing agent)?

1149. Has your organization taken a well-grounded decision about the procurement procedure chosen and has it documented the process?

1150. Is it tested periodically, whether your organizations way of handling tasks is competitive in relation to price and quality?

1151. Are goods generally ordered and received in time to be used in the programs for which they were ordered?

1152. Are approval limits definitive as to amount and classification of expenditure?

1153. Are receiving reports on file for all claims for equipment, supplies and materials in the paid claims file?

1154. Are controls proportionated to risks?

1155. Were calculations used in evaluation adequate and correct?

1156. Are cases of double payment duly prevented and corrected?

1157. Was the submission of variant tenders accepted and duly ruled?

5.2 Contract Close-Out: Security Consultants

1158. Have all contracts been closed?

1159. Change in circumstances?

1160. Change in knowledge?

1161. Parties: Authorized?

1162. How does it work?

1163. Was the contract sufficiently clear so as not to result in numerous disputes and misunderstandings?

1164. Why Outsource?

1165. Was the contract complete without requiring numerous changes and revisions?

1166. Parties: who is involved?

1167. How is the contracting office notified of the automatic contract close-out?

1168. Have all acceptance criteria been met prior to final payment to contractors?

1169. Have all contracts been completed?

1170. Change in attitude or behavior?

1171. How/when used ?

1172. Are the signers the authorized officials?

1173. Was the contract type appropriate?

1174. What is capture management?

1175. What happens to the recipient of services?

1176. Have all contract records been included in the Security Consultants project archives?

1177. Has each contract been audited to verify acceptance and delivery?

5.3 Project or Phase Close-Out: Security Consultants

1178. Were the outcomes different from the already stated planned?

1179. Is the lesson based on actual Security Consultants project experience rather than on independent research?

1180. Did the Security Consultants project management methodology work?

1181. Were messages directly related to the release strategy or phases of the Security Consultants project?

1182. Does the lesson describe a function that would be done differently the next time?

1183. What was expected from each stakeholder?

1184. In preparing the Lessons Learned report, should it reflect a consensus viewpoint, or should the report reflect the different individual viewpoints?

1185. Who are the Security Consultants project stakeholders and what are roles and involvement?

1186. Which changes might a stakeholder be required to make as a result of the Security Consultants project?

1187. Is there a clear cause and effect between the activity and the lesson learned?

1188. Who controlled key decisions that were made?

1189. Can the lesson learned be replicated?

1190. What is this stakeholder expecting?

1191. Who exerted influence that has positively affected or negatively impacted the Security Consultants project?

1192. What information did each stakeholder need to contribute to the Security Consultants projects success?

1193. How often did each stakeholder need an update?

1194. What can you do better next time, and what specific actions can you take to improve?

5.4 Lessons Learned: Security Consultants

1195. What were the lessons learned on this Security Consultants project?

1196. Whom to share Lessons Learned Information with?

1197. What could have been improved?

1198. For the next Security Consultants project, how could you improve on the way Security Consultants project was conducted?

1199. How well defined were the acceptance criteria for Security Consultants project deliverables?

1200. Was the Security Consultants project manager sufficiently experienced, skilled, trained, supported?

1201. How does the budget cycle affect the case?

1202. How many government and contractor personnel are authorized for the Security Consultants project?

1203. How comprehensive was integration testing?

1204. What regulatory regime controlled how your organization head and program manager directed your organization and Security Consultants project?

1205. How effective were your functional specs?

1206. How effective was Security Consultants project Team member training?

1207. How spontaneous are the communications?

1208. What were the main bottlenecks on the process?

1209. Who is responsible for each action?

1210. What on the Security Consultants project worked well and was effective in the delivery of the product?

1211. What data are likely to be missing?

1212. How well do you feel the executives supported this Security Consultants project?

1213. Was the control overhead justified?

1214. How much communication is task-related?

Index

CPSIA information can be obtained
at www.ICGtesting.com
Printed in the USA
BVHW041223110719
553191BV00015B/1304/P

9 780655 813248